The Google Infused Classroom
A Guidebook to Making Thinking Visible and Amplifying Student Voice
By Holly Clark and Tanya Avrith

This beautifully designed book offers guidance on using technology to design instruction that allows students to show their thinking, demonstrate their learning, and share their work (and voices!) with authentic audiences. The Google Infused Classroom will equip you to empower your students to use technology in meaningful ways that prepare them for the future.

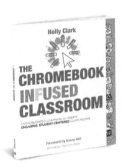

The Chromebook Infused Classroom
Using Blended Learning to Create Engaging, Student-Centered Classrooms
By Holly Clark

Whether Chromebooks are a new addition to your school, or you have recently gone 1:1 in the classroom, or have been using them for years and you want to make the most of technology for your learners. The Chromebook Infused Classroom is a resource you will want to refer to again and again.

The Microsoft Infused Classroom
A Guidebook to Making Thinking Visible and Amplifying Student Voice
By Holly Clark

Looking for ways to create a student-centered classroom and make your lessons come alive? The Microsoft Infused Classroom has the answers! Designed to help you amplify teaching and engagement in your classroom, The Microsoft Infused Classroom equips you to use powerful tools that put learning first!

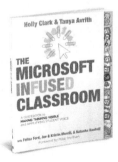

THE AI INFUSED CLASSROOM

INSPIRING IDEAS TO **SHIFT TEACHING** AND **MAXIMIZE MEANINGFUL LEARNING** IN THE **WORLD** OF **AI**

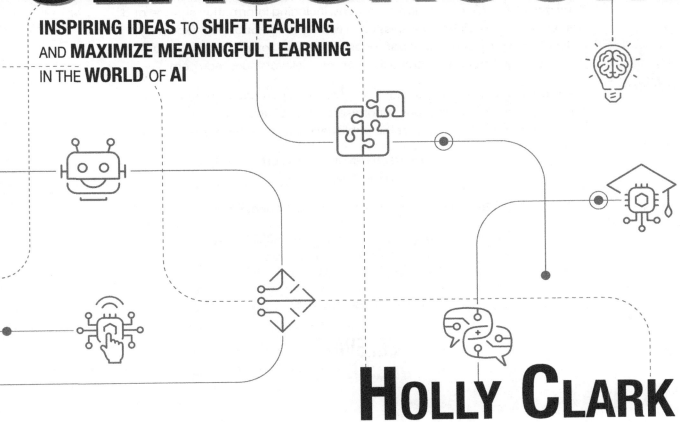

HOLLY CLARK

This book is available at special discounts when purchased in quantity for use as premiums, promotions, fundraisers, or for educational purposes. For inquiries and details, contact the publisher: info@elevatebooksedu.com.

Published by Elevate Books EDU
Del Mar, California

Editing and Design by My Writers' Connection

Library of Congress Control Number: 2023938107
Paperback ISBN: 979-8-9851374-5-3
Ebook ISBN: 979-8-9851374-6-0

First Printing: May 2023

Contents

How Much Did ChatGPT Help Me Write This Book?

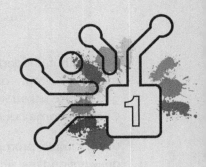

It's the question every educator should be asking: *How much did ChatGPT help write this?*

I know you may be wondering the same thing about this book. You may also be asking questions like these:

- ◉ What are the strengths and weaknesses of artificial intelligence (AI) models, like ChatGPT?
- ◉ How does ChatGPT help with or change the writing process?
- ◉ What do educators need to understand about what language models like this can do to transform our ability to get a message across in a more time-sensitive manner?
- ◉ How can we teach students to use AI appropriately and in ways that enhance their learning experiences?

Open-source, content-creating AI models are a relatively new addition to the education landscape, but they are simply the next step in edtech tools. With more than twenty-five years in education and as one of the first educators in the United States to have a 1:1 classroom, my approach to technology integration has always been future-oriented. I know that by focusing on the deep learning and masterful pedagogy we can achieve with educational shifts (like the one we are currently experiencing), we can create and broaden meaningful learning experiences for our students.

It's from that point of view that I wrote this book. The ideas in *The AI Infused Classroom* come from my own and others' classroom practices and from extensive research and study, including insights I gained during my National Board Certification and master's program.

And, yes, I used ChatGPT during the writing process. Here's how:

When it came to writing, I started out old-school. I wrote the first draft, either by typing or using voice-to-text. After refining and editing my ideas, I pasted paragraphs that needed help into ChatGPT and requested suggestions for improvements by simply asking, "Can you make this better?" The results were quite good. I also asked whether I had missed any details that should be included, and ChatGPT came back with suggested additions.

Using simple prompts, like the following, helped me ensure I got the kind of answers and results I needed:

Can you check this piece for logical thought organization?

Please don't shorten this piece. Keep the regular length and just add more compelling word choices.

Here is a piece of my writing. Can you take this style and rewrite the section above using my voice?

Is there anything missing that would make my ideas more clear?

Can you please stop using transition statements and rewrite the ideas above? (LOL, I actually said, "please.")

Play devil's advocate. Is there anything wrong with these ideas?

Can you expand on this train of thought?

Can you clean this up and make it more appealing to the reader?

Is there any other research on AI literacies that I did not include?

How can I make this more clear?

What title would you give this if it were a chapter in a book?

Using conversational prompts and questions like these made the process feel as if I were leaning over and talking to a human next to me. I tried more technical prompts, but the results weren't better or more profound. (It felt good to drop the formalities.)

Each time I completed a chapter, I put it into ChatGPT and asked for further recommendations. I also asked the program to analyze the chapter's strengths and weaknesses and how I might improve the flow and writing to make my book more accessible to you, the reader. Sometimes the suggestions were awe-inspiring; other times they were simple synonyms and unimpressive.

ChatGPT was great at enhancing my writing overall, but it sometimes replaced my word choice with less fitting synonyms or created listicles when they weren't needed. (These lists happened more with ChatGPT 4 than with 3.5.) I had to keep reminding the language model not to condense the writing too much, as it tended to minimize details. And although it occasionally overused words, ChatGPT masterfully blended my thoughts with its suggestions.

 Note: I added the same ideas and used similar prompts in Google Bard, and was consistently unimpressed with the result. (I should note, however, that Google Bard had only been available for three days.)

Paragraph by paragraph and chapter by chapter, I edited and then compared my last draft to ChatGPT's final recommendations. Interestingly, every time I instructed the AI to rewrite a section, it generated a version that was different from the previous one. Even if I gave the AI the *same prompt* for improvements on a piece, its revised copy was unique and distinct—meaning it never gave me the same suggestions twice.

I also used ChatGPT to verify my research, which proved to be a tremendous time-saver. When writing about the Question Formulation Technique, for instance, ChatGPT quickly confirmed the accuracy of the steps I had outlined.

Working with ChatGPT to write this book felt like having a writing assistant, instant editor, and respected advisor working alongside me. It saved an incredible amount of time. In comparison, my first book, *The Google Infused Classroom*, took more than a year to complete with a co-author. With ChatGPT as my virtual co-author, I dedicated twelve-hour days to this new book, worked through the weekends, and finished in record time.

Working with ChatGPT to write this book felt like having a writing assistant, instant editor, and respected advisor working alongside me.

So, that's the story of how I *wrote The AI Infused Classroom* so quickly. Now, this AI-infused book will go to a professional team of (human) editors and a layout artist (also human) for production. In a matter of a few weeks, this book will be available to educators everywhere.

The time-saving benefits of AI models, like ChatGPT, make it invaluable. As does its ability to enhance ideas and expand creative visions, ensure accuracy, find sources, double-check research, and improve the clarity and quality of writing.

And it's only the beginning of the AI revolution. The possibilities are truly astounding.

Where Did That Robot Come From?

In 2018, I visited an innovative school just outside Beijing, China, to speak about infusing edtech in the classroom. The trip offered a shocking glimpse into the future and how technology, specifically robots, would soon change our world.

As I checked into my hotel, a robot scanned my app, assigned me a room, and handed me a key. On the way to my room, I noticed little R2-D2-style robots effortlessly buzzing up and down the corridors. They zipped in and out of elevators as they helped guests with their needs and delivered items to their rooms.

At first, interacting with these metallic creatures felt jarring—a bit too futuristic. Soon, however, seeing robots everywhere became routine. I even found myself holding the elevator door for them as they went about their tasks, almost forgetting that they weren't human.

On the long flight home, I reflected on the incredible advancement and use of technology I'd seen in China. The robots had seamlessly integrated into the hotel's operations. Even more interesting, the technology had become *normal* to me during my short stay. It was unlike anything I had ever encountered in the United States or anywhere else for that matter. China, after all, with its massive population, has access to vast amounts of data—data that could be used to create incredibly sophisticated artificial intelligence.

This TikTok shows a room service robot at another hotel in Beijing. (They don't actually sound like R2-D2)

The surreal, eye-opening experience made me consider how this new technology might one day impact education. These little robots were only the beginning of what was to come in our rapidly changing world. What else might we see in the next five to twenty years? And how could these advancements improve learners' experiences?

Intrigued by the possibilities, I dove into the world of AI, taking in everything I could about this new technology. I set up a Google alert and read whatever I could find about AI's latest developments and emerging technologies. I also bought my first book about AI: *AI Super Powers*: *China, Silicon Valley, and the New World Order* by Kai-Fu Lee, a Taiwanese computer scientist and business leader who has created and overseen technological advancements in machine learning for several of the world's major tech companies, including Google, Apple, and Microsoft.

The more I learned, the more I became convinced that AI was going to transform our world in ways we couldn't even imagine. Kai-Fu Lee affirmed my suspicion during an interview on *60 Minutes* in 2019:

Scan the QR code to watch the segment.

Scott Pelley: "I wonder, do you think people around the world have any idea what's coming with Artificial intelligence?"

Kai-Fu Lee: "I think most people have no idea, and many people have the wrong idea."

Scott Pelley: "But you do think it's going to change the world?"

Kai-Fu Lee: "I think it's going to change the world more than anything in the history of mankind. More than electricity. More than the Industrial Revolution. It's going to be transformative in ways that we can't even imagine."

One year later . . .

When the global pandemic hit in 2020, the world went into lockdown. Day-to-day, most of us turned our focus to important things like trying to stay healthy and mastering our new at-home lifestyles. I couldn't help but wonder, though, about the AI advancements that were probably being developed while we watched COVID-19 case reports and the presidential debates on our televisions and devices. I told my friends and family that it was only a matter of time before AI would hit us fast and furious. Indeed, while we were preoccupied with masks and vaccines, a transformer at Google was up to something big (more on that shortly).

Learning More about AI

After I visited China, I added content—and warnings—about AI to my keynotes and training sessions. But back in 2018 and 2019, most educators weren't ready to listen. It was hard for many people (not just educators) to imagine that robots and intuitive computer programs could soon be a reality for everyday life. After all, AI was something we saw in futuristic movies, not in the classroom.

That attitude changed in early 2023, however, when a *generative pretrained transformer* (GPT) hit the scene with the ability to speak not just computer code but *human* languages. What we now know as ChatGPT from OpenAI forever changed the future—and the present.

Dismissing or even denying the potential of technology is understandable. Humans tend to stay focused on the present. That's been true for decades, despite the exponential advancements our world has seen in the past century. Few of my middle school and high school teachers, for example, could have imagined that we would one day have access to an internet's worth of information or that we would be able to voice-type papers on computers or *smartphones.* Did those teachers get me ready for this future? I can't say they all did. But I'm so grateful for the teachers who taught me to be a curious learner. By encouraging me to look around and look ahead and to ask questions—*Why? How? What are the possibilities?* and *For what purpose?*—those teachers did their jobs right!

This book is dedicated to that kind of teacher. The teachers who, instead of saying *no* to using ChatGPT and other AI in the classroom, are saying *Tell me more.*

The robots in my Beijing hotel reminded me that the world is changing rapidly and that we must adapt and innovate to keep up. My curiosity—the same curiosity that those forward-thinking teachers fostered in me—made me want to know more about the AI that made those little robots work.

The fact that you're reading this book is an indication that you're at least a little bit curious too.

What is artificial intelligence and how does it work?

Let's start with a few definitions to help us understand the technology that is changing the world.

Artificial intelligence (AI) is an umbrella term for a group of technologies that enable computers to perform tasks that typically require human intelligence.

Two important AI models to be aware of are human-trained AI and deep-learning AI.

Human-trained AI

Human-trained AI involves developing algorithms, models, and techniques that enable machines to simulate human-like cognitive abilities and make intelligent decisions based on data and patterns.

Examples of human-trained AI include tech tools and uses that you may already be using, such as email filtering and autonomous vehicles. My robot friends in Beijing operated with human-trained AI. Someone programmed them to perform specific tasks at the hotel—and the robots

I'm so grateful for the teachers who taught me to be a curious learner. By encouraging me to look around and look ahead and to ask questions— *Why? How? What are the possibilities?* and *For what purpose?*—those teachers did their jobs right!

This book is dedicated to that kind of teacher.

did them impressively well! If a guest requested more towels, the robot loaded up, got on the elevator, and delivered fresh towels to their room.

Deep-learning AI

Deep-learning AI uses artificial neural networks that allow machines to learn from data and then perform tasks without being explicitly programmed. These artificial neural networks simulate the human brain's ability to take in information (albeit in very large datasets) and use that data to learn and make decisions. Deep-learning AI can make complex decisions and perform complicated tasks.

Examples of deep-learning AI in action include facial recognition (used by everyone from the FBI to Facebook) and language translation (think Google Translate).

Stated simply, human-trained AI can only perform tasks it has been specifically programmed to do. Deep-learning AI can learn and adapt to new situations, making it more versatile and powerful than its counterpart.

Deep-learning AI has incredible potential. Its uses, however, were limited (at least for a while) because it was difficult for humans to understand how this AI works, which made effective communication challenging.

So, what's changed?

Developers have been hard at work, creating an easier way for humans and machines to talk to one another. It's called *natural language processing*. They've also been developing more effective and efficient ways for AI to take in data, decipher it, and then make informed and independent decisions using *large language models*. These are two terms that come up frequently when discussing AI, so you'll want to understand and remember them. Let's take a closer look at each.

Natural Language Processing

Programmers have been working on natural language processing (NLP) since the 1950s. It hasn't been until more recent years, however, that the uses of NLP moved from the computer lab to the consumer arena. Today, NLP helps to bridge the gap between machines and everyday users like you and me by allowing computers to understand and interpret human language.

In simple terms, NLP enables humans to communicate with AI naturally and intuitively. Remember what I said about the prompts I gave to ChatGPT? I didn't use technical terms or complicated code. I gave directions and asked questions just as I would have if I had been speaking to a human. NLP made that possible.

NLP is crucial for the development of AI applications such as virtual assistants, chatbots, and language translation services. It uses a combination of machine learning, linguistics, and computational techniques to analyze and understand human language, including its syntax, semantics, and pragmatics.

The potential uses of NLP for educators include automated essay grading, plagiarism detection, personalized learning assistance, and language tutoring. Imagine how any one of those applications could save you time or multiply your efforts.

Large Language Model (LLM)

NLP is what allows AI to understand you. Large language models (LLM) are what enable AI to talk back to you in terms that you can understand.

An LLM is a subset or type of deep-learning AI. The model uses extensive amounts of text data to learn how to generate human-like responses to natural language queries. That data can come from almost anywhere, including books, articles, social media posts, transcripts, or research findings.

LLMs rely on the artificial neural networks I mentioned earlier to process and use information. The AI can then make decisions based on the data it has accumulated, mimicking the way your brain takes in, evaluates, and uses new information in light of your existing knowledge.

WARNING:
Be mindful of potential biases and limitations in LLMs. Don't rely solely on AI when making critical educational decisions.

You've probably chatted with LLMs numerous times. You just didn't call them that. Chatbots, like those helpful (and sometimes annoying) virtual assistants that pop up while you're shopping online, are powered by LLMs. They use the information they've gathered to anticipate and answer questions. ChatGPT and Google Bard, likewise, function using a version of LLMs.

As a teacher, you might find LLMs useful in various educational contexts, such as providing instant feedback to students, supporting research through efficient information retrieval, and offering supplementary learning materials based on the model's vast knowledge.

Where did robots, ChatGPT, and other AI come from?

The timeline that follows provides an overview of some of the major developments since 2017.

2017 The Google Transformer

- Two years before my interaction with those robots, engineers in the Google Brain lab were developing technology that would change our world. The lab was founded in 2011 to explore deep-learning algorithms and neural networks. To that end, engineers were working on a transformer that would use deep learning the way our human brains do to solve complex problems. The goal wasn't to create a robot but a brain of sorts that could use language to answer bigger questions than humans could alone.

- This kind of deep learning first required training, so the engineers loaded the transformer with a bunch of data. They hoped the transformer would make its outputs based on their inputs. And it did!

- The transform excelled at sequential data. Engineers could input a question, and it would respond with what it *thought* was the response you wanted.

- Something called a self-attention mechanism made this *thinking* possible. It was what allowed the transformer to take into account the context of each word in a sentence when generating new text.

- While the Google Transformer was not specifically designed to answer questions or provide responses to human input, its capabilities in handling sequential data paved the way for the development of LLMs, like GPT.

2018 OpenAI develops GPT-1

- In 2018, researchers at OpenAI created a new language model called GPT-1 (Generative pre-trained transformer).

- GPT-1 was trained on a massive amount of text data and was able to generate coherent and contextually appropriate text in response to prompts.

2020 OpenAI released a new language model called ChatGPT

- This new model was designed to generate text that mimics human conversation.
- It was trained on a massive dataset of human-written text and learned to generate natural-sounding and engaging responses to prompts.
- It showed a wide range of potential applications, including virtual assistants, chatbots, and customer service tools.
- Its ability to generate natural and contextually appropriate responses made it a powerful tool for enhancing communication and collaboration between humans and machines.

2022 ChatGPT is released.

- In November, OpenAI released ChatGPT.

2023 Everything changes.

- By January 2023, ChatGPT had more than 100 million active users, and that number is still growing.

Today, teachers everywhere are asking questions about this new technology!

Interacting with robots in China gave me a peek into what the future might hold. Even so, I never imagined the breakthroughs that would show up on my computer screen only four years later. Now we can talk to machines! They help me with my daily routines, and even helped me write this book!

What does AI mean for education?

Let's investigate.

The Shift in
Information and Writing

If you're teaching our youngest students, you're educating children who will graduate from high school and college in the mid-2030s and beyond. These same students, as adults, will work for approximately fifty years (as the retirement age shifts) and eventually retire around 2085.

Pause for a moment and let that sink in. They'll retire in 2085—in a future we can barely imagine.

Many classrooms, however, fail to adequately prepare students for this future. Instead, schools tend to be structured by traditional teaching methods that were popularized nearly a century ago.

Our learners are already living in a world filled with AI and continual technological advancements. If we don't equip them to thrive in this ever-changing world, we are essentially stifling their potential. Sure, they'll learn how to navigate the new technology eventually. But imagine the possibilities if they discovered how to use it well—to their educational advantage (rather than trying to use it to skip learning) and for the benefit of those around them. That's what I want for our kids, and I'm sure you do too.

So how do we equip kids to thrive today and tomorrow? We start by acknowledging where we are and where we're going. Throughout history, there have been several major shifts in information and the ways we access, store, and share it.

But *this* is different.

Until now, we've witnessed a gradual unfolding of technological progress. Today, *as we teach*, a large-scale shift is happening—at a much faster pace than we expected.

And there's no stopping it.

So we have a choice: Stick our heads in the sand and hope for the best, or *make* the best use of the amazing innovations at our fingertips.

Until now, we've witnessed a gradual unfolding of technological progress. Today, *as we teach*, a large-scale shift is happening—at a much faster pace than we expected.

And there's no stopping it.

So we have a choice: Stick our heads in the sand and hope for the best, or *make* the best use of the amazing innovations at our fingertips.

Information Exchange: Where We Started and Where We're Headed

(I partnered with ChatGPT for this section. It just did a better job than me alone.)

Let's take a look at some of those major shifts in the way we access and use information, starting with the shift that allowed us to collect and pass along information in a tangible format.

Oral tradition to written language
The development of written language allowed people to record and share information, preserving knowledge for future generations.

Manuscripts to the printing press
The invention of the printing press by Johannes Gutenberg in the mid-fifteenth century revolutionized the way information was disseminated. It enabled the mass production of books, making them more accessible and affordable, which in turn facilitated the spread of ideas and learning.

Analog to digital technology
Digital technology has a profound impact on the way we acquire and distribute information. Digital data can be stored more efficiently, accessed more easily, and shared instantly across vast distances.

Libraries and card catalogs to online databases
Physical libraries and card catalogs have been replaced with digital databases and search engines that allow users to find and access information quickly and easily from anywhere with an internet connection.

Encyclopedias to Wikipedia and other online resources
Print encyclopedias have been supplanted by online resources, like Wikipedia, which offers vast repositories of information that can be updated and edited by users in real time.

Remember this? Wikipedia brought on our first collective educational freak-out. Now the site is a widely accepted place to start researching information.

Desktop computers to mobile devices

The shift from desktop computers to mobile devices, such as smartphones and tablets, has made information even more accessible, allowing users to access the internet and digital resources on the go.

Physical storage to cloud storage

The move from physical storage media like CDs, DVDs, and hard drives to cloud-based storage solutions enables users to store and access data remotely, making it easier to share and collaborate on projects.

Evolving from traditional programming to a choose-your-own media approach

The rise of the internet and streaming services has allowed users to consume media content in a non-linear fashion, enabling them to choose what they watch, listen to, or read, and when.

Social media and user-generated content

Platforms like Facebook, Twitter, Instagram, and YouTube have shifted the way we share and consume information. User-generated content plays a significant role in shaping public discourse and opinion.

Internet searching to AI bots...

Ready or not, this is where we are headed. *How will we as educators respond to this shift?*

Students' Needs Are Also Changing

As technology continues to change our world, we are seeing a significant shift in our students and the way they learn. We are now moving from Gen Z kids, with their eight-second attention spans, to Alpha Gen, a generation of learners who not only desire but also demand more personalized and engaging learning experiences. Alpha Gen includes students born after 2010, and they are sure to require us to shift our teaching and learning ideas to meet their needs.

The Alpha Generation's Rule-Breaking Approach

The Alpha Generation's digital proficiency enables them to delve deeply into various subjects and learn from diverse perspectives and genuine experts through platforms like YouTube. As a result, they may challenge conventional methods and ideas.

Demand for Personalized Learning Experiences

This generation seeks tailored learning experiences, as they are aware that easily accessible information is just a query away via Alexa, Google, or ChatGPT. With encouragement and support, they can exhibit greater self-direction in their learning than previous generations did.

Seamless Integration with Technology

Alpha Gen students are characterized by a virtually seamless relationship with technology. It is estimated that, by the age of eight, they will surpass their parents and teachers in technological skills. This inherent connection to technology shapes their approach to learning, communication, and problem-solving.

AI in the Classroom

AI provides us with an incredible opportunity to make personalized learning a reality. Rather than viewing it as a tool for students to cheat, we can shift our perspective and embrace AI as a means for teachers to create engaging learning experiences that were previously impossible due to time constraints.

The teachers who are willing to embrace AI have the opportunity and power to transform their classrooms into vibrant hubs of learning. They can use it to inspire students to become lifelong learners by diving into fascinating inquiry- and problem-based learning projects. These educators will learn how to use AI to make each lesson captivating and memorable. In doing so, they will equip their students with the skills and knowledge they'll need to thrive in a rapidly changing world.

In other classrooms, instruction will remain anchored in traditional teaching methods, with packets of worksheets and teacher-centered instruction that focuses on details rather than big ideas. Students will continue to sit in neat rows, waiting for knowledge to be imparted.

We can't continue to employ teaching strategies from 1985 to prepare students for a world that's a century ahead in 2085.

My hope in writing this book was to inspire a different approach. One that thoughtfully addresses the opportunities before us and the changing needs of our students.

Let's Start with the Elephant in the Room: ChatGPT

When most people (parents, educators, administrators, and even the general public) think of ChatGPT, they assume it's a tool that students will use to cheat on their writing assignments. The fear is that students will use it as a shortcut, and that writing as we know it will be a thing of the past.

To be fair, that isn't an ungrounded assumption. It has already happened enough that *South Park* created an episode titled "Deep Learning" that perfectly captures the dilemma. In the episode, *South Park* students suddenly start submitting high-quality papers—something Mr. Garrison, their teacher, has never seen from some of his students.

With the shift in information caused by ChatGPT, it's not surprising that I hear this question every day:

Scan the QR code to enjoy a quick laugh.

Will we be able to detect whether students have used ChatGPT to cheat?

It is a fair question, but *it is the wrong question.*

- It is anchored in the old-school, 1985 pedagogy that every student must learn to write in a certain way.
- It assumes students can only learn to write effectively through the continuous practice of putting words on paper—and that they must do this by themselves and with the help of feedback from the teacher.
- And interestingly, the question ignores the axiom that *to become a good writer, one must be an avid reader.*

Significant shifts in information transfer often ignite cautionary reactions. Socrates, for example, doubted the efficacy of writing as a means of conveying knowledge. He believed face-to-face communication was the sole method by which knowledge could accurately be transferred from one person to another. What he didn't realize was that oral and written communication could coexist and were each uniquely valuable.

Socrates wasn't ready for it, but the shift went on, and writing became an acceptable, even essential, form of communication. Just like many people today, he was hesitant to embrace the shift. But it is coming; in fact, it's here, and it's forcing us to acknowledge that reading, writing, and editing are inextricably linked. All are uniquely valuable and each one can support the growth of the other.

English Language Arts teacher Jill Pavich emphasizes that academic writing is only *one* part of the broader writing landscape. Fundamentally, writing is about communication—conveying information in a clear, coherent, and well-organized manner. Skilled writers must grasp the intricacies of language, appreciate examples of impactful word choice, recognize the art of wordplay, and observe how similes convey meaning. Often, these writing skills are developed as students practice reading and editing. They are then honed as learners put the insights they've gained into practice by writing, evaluating feedback, and refining their work.

We find ourselves in a situation similar to the one Socrates struggled with. Except this time, those words he was afraid of are being generated by a non-human. It is a big shift to wrap your head around.

How can our writing skills co-exist with AI?

As we navigate this transformative period in our understanding of writing, it's essential to take a moment and think deeply about the multifaceted nature of the writing process. Writing is bound to evolve, and while we may be tempted to resist change and focus on preventing students from cheating, such concerns only tether us to outdated perspectives. Instead, we must prioritize our students' futures by exploring how we can harness these groundbreaking writing tools to elicit even better written work from them.

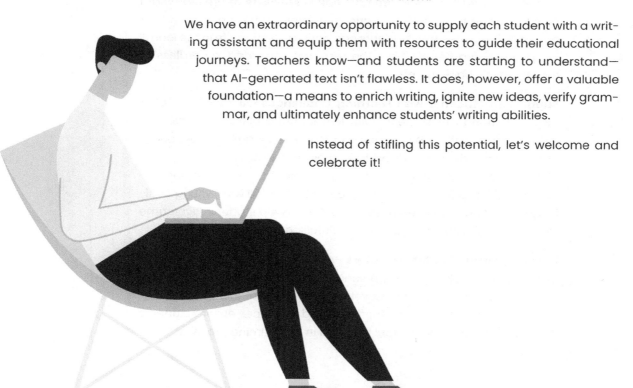

We have an extraordinary opportunity to supply each student with a writing assistant and equip them with resources to guide their educational journeys. Teachers know—and students are starting to understand—that AI-generated text isn't flawless. It does, however, offer a valuable foundation—a means to enrich writing, ignite new ideas, verify grammar, and ultimately enhance students' writing abilities.

Instead of stifling this potential, let's welcome and celebrate it!

AI Models Can Be the Great Equalizer

AI can help educators level the playing field for all learners. These tools provide us with an unprecedented opportunity to bridge gaps in education and create more equitable access to resources and learning experiences.

How? Here are six ways.

Broadening Horizons—AI tools can give students access to ideas and resources they may not have been exposed to because of their location or socioeconomic background.

Expanding Vocabulary—They empower students to expand their vocabularies by exposing them to words they might not have heard, seen, or mastered yet due to language differences or learning struggles. By offering real-time translation, suggesting synonyms, and providing context-specific definitions, these tools allow students to better understand and use complex or unfamiliar words.

Breaking Down Language Barriers—AI-powered tools break down language barriers by providing instant translations of text or speech. This enables students who are non-native speakers or are learning a new language to access educational content in their preferred language. This ensures that students can actively participate in the learning process and benefit from the resources provided, regardless of their linguistic background.

Supporting Students with Learning Challenges—AI tools can offer targeted support to students with learning difficulties, such as dyslexia, ADHD, or autism, by providing personalized learning experiences and accommodations that address their unique needs. For example, AI-powered text-to-speech tools can help students with reading difficulties, while speech-to-text tools can assist those with writing challenges. By offering tailored assistance, AI can help students overcome their learning struggles and reach their full potential.

Curating Resources for Educators—AI empowers educators to efficiently create inclusive and personalized learning experiences. Using AI, teachers can curate and develop learning materials that are culturally relevant and diverse. These tailored resources ensure students from various backgrounds feel included in the learning process.

Fostering Collaboration Locally and Beyond—LLMs can facilitate communication and collaboration among students from diverse backgrounds by providing translation and interpretation tools that enable real-time interaction in multiple languages. Not only does this foster a sense of belonging and connection, but it also helps students develop valuable skills, such as empathy, problem-solving, and teamwork—all of which are crucial for success in a globalized world.

AI tools can empower students with diverse backgrounds, languages, and learning struggles to thrive in the classroom. By harnessing the power of AI, we can work toward creating a more equitable and inclusive educational landscape that benefits all learners.

Shifts in information, and access to that information, have consistently served as powerful equalizers, facilitating the democratization of learning throughout history. Once again, we find ourselves in a transformative place. To ensure a bright future for our students, we must embrace this shift with open minds.

Infusing ChatGPT and AI into the Writing Process

You can always edit a bad page.
You can't edit a blank page.

—Jodi Picoult

Imagine this: It's a typical Friday morning, and your students are dragging into the classroom. But instead of starting the day with your usual writing prompts, you surprise them with an AI-generated prompt:

I am interested in space exploration; what are 10 interesting ideas about the future of space travel?

Suddenly, the room is abuzz with chatter as students brainstorm, throwing out wild and imaginative ideas.

The creative experience doesn't stop there. Using AI tools, students collaborate on a story, with each person contributing a sentence or paragraph and the AI suggesting alternatives. Your students learn together as the AI-generated responses expand their vocabulary with new words and phrases.

Next, you have your students dive deeper into their writing practice. This time they turn to AI tools for research assistance. The LLM summarizes articles and extracts key information from a variety of sites and resources. Of course, you reminded your students to ask the AI to cite the sources it has pulled from. The task improves both their research efficiency and their comprehension of the material.

Finally, you have your students proofread their work. This step includes using AI tools to check their grammar and the clarity of their writing. At the same time, they learn the importance of exercising their judgment in the editing process. After all, sometimes the AI gets it wrong.

The New World of Writing

I have already seen the incredible potential of LLMs at work in the classroom. Brave and curious teachers are using AI tools to spark students' imaginations. This technology, when used intentionally, is stretching our learners' creativity and expanding their academic abilities.

Increased creativity and inspiration are valuable (and fun) perks of using AI as an integral part of the writing process, but those benefits are only the beginning.

Think about the essential skills students need to learn and develop:

- Critical reading
- Critical thinking
- Persuasive communication
- The ability to identify and differentiate the characteristics of various types of writing

Now consider how you might employ AI tools to challenge your students to strengthen these skills. For instance, they could use AI-generated examples as mentor texts to understand the structure, organization, and characteristics of various genres and types of writing.

It's easy and effective to use AI as a starting-point tool for a variety of writing assignments. You can provide (or ask students to collect) AI-generated text or prompts to spark ideas for poems, short stories, or essays. The point, of course, is to challenge students to build upon or draw from AI-generated content to create original works.

When it comes to critical reading and thinking skills, you might have students evaluate AI-generated text to identify strengths, weaknesses, and potential biases. Or you might add a persuasive writing element by asking students to use an LLM to generate opposing viewpoints on specific topics. With those pieces, they can then draft persuasive arguments.

Another option for developing critical reading and thinking skills is to use AI-generated summaries of news articles as a starting point for choosing a research topic. Students can explore new topics and perspectives and then identify potential biases. They might ask an LLM to test the summaries for accuracy and the credibility of sources. Armed with this information, students can determine which concepts need further research.

It's easy and effective to use AI as a starting-point tool for a variety of writing assignments. You can provide (or ask students to collect) AI-generated text or prompts to spark ideas for poems, short stories, or essays. The point, of course, is to challenge students to build upon or draw from AI-generated content to create original works.

And as they reflect on their writing journey, they turn to AI tools for journaling, with the AI providing suggestions or prompts to help them process their thoughts and what they've learned.

In the words of Jodi Picoult, "You can always edit a bad page. You can't edit a blank page." With the power of ChatGPT and AI, we can ensure that our students never face a blank page again.

Evaluating the Purpose of Writing

Shifting our ideas about writing in a world of AI requires that we reconsider our understanding of writing. We must ask questions we may have taken for granted even one year ago. Questions like, **What is writing?** and **What do students need to learn from, with, or about writing?**

At its core, writing is about communication. That hasn't changed. What *has* changed is that successful communication is far more complex and multifaceted than the simple acts of putting text on paper or typing words on a screen.

Think about your own reading experiences. Reading today involves a rich tapestry of images, videos, and interactive elements alongside written text. For students to thrive as communicators, we must incorporate this layered, multimedia approach to our teaching of writing.

ISTE
Student Standards

It's also important to recognize that academic writing is only one facet of the broader communication spectrum. The ISTE student standards provide learning goals we should be working toward with our students. Those goals are to see students become empowered learners, good digital citizens, knowledge constructors, innovative designers, computational thinkers, creative communicators, and global collaborators. When we equip and encourage them to meet these standards, we are preparing them to share their voices capably and confidently now and as they move through the remainder of their academic careers and into the marketplace.

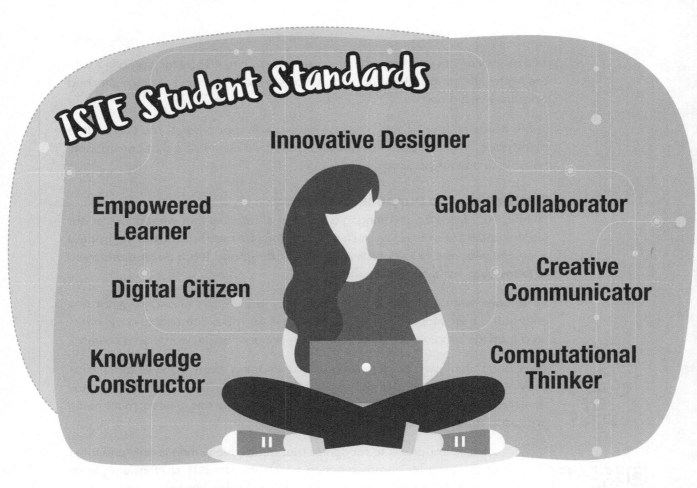

ISTE Student Standards

Innovative Designer

Empowered Learner

Global Collaborator

Digital Citizen

Creative Communicator

Knowledge Constructor

Computational Thinker

Although only one of these standards includes the word *communicator*, communication is a vital aspect of each one. With that in mind, we *must* encourage students to explore various mediums and forms of expression, including storytelling, multimedia presentations, and digital art. By doing so, we are equipping students with the skills they will need to tackle the challenges and opportunities presented by an increasingly interconnected and technologically-driven world.

Improving Students' Communication Skills with *Layered* Writing Assignments

If our goal is to equip learners to become successful communicators, writing is only one element (albeit a vital element) of modern writing assignments. Requiring students to infuse their work with multimedia elements teaches them to effectively convey their ideas. Consider using one or more of the following questions to create layered writing assignments:

What images help explain this?

Students can use relevant images, diagrams, or charts to support their arguments, and provide visual examples, to help readers better understand the concepts being discussed.

What's the elevator pitch for this?

Ask students to develop a brief, compelling summary of their main ideas or arguments using relevant keywords. (Keywords are words and phrases that someone might use when searching a topic.) This exercise can help students refine their focus, clarify their thinking, and improve their message. In the real world, this kind of writing is regularly used for blog summaries and in marketing content and sales presentations.

How would a graphic or infographic help the reader visualize the ideas?

Students could create visual aids, such as infographics to help readers quickly grasp complex ideas, data, or processes. These graphics could illustrate key concepts, relationships, or comparisons.

Would it benefit from being read by the author?

When students record an audio narration of their work, they provide an additional layer of accessibility and personal connection for their audience. This process helps them identify where their writing might be unclear and find typos and grammar mistakes.

How would you condense this into a short video, emphasizing the takeaways you want people to remember?

Students can produce a concise video that highlights the main points of their work, using engaging visuals and animations to emphasize the key takeaways. This exercise can help them develop storytelling and presentation skills as well as reinforce their understanding of the material.

Would this benefit from an illustration?

Encourage students to create original illustrations or artwork to accompany their writing. These visual elements can enhance the reader's experience, provide additional context, and showcase students' creativity and artistic talents.

Improving Students' Communication Skills with AI-Infused Writing

I hope you've already begun to consider ways that you can incorporate AI as a learning tool for your students. Using ChatGPT isn't (or doesn't have to be) about *cheating* or having the computer do all the work. Employed effectively, it can help students expand their ideas, bring their creativity to life, and improve the quality of their work. The following ideas are a few ways you might encourage students to use ChatGPT in your AI-infused writing assignments.

For Feedback—Students can ask ChatGPT for feedback by using prompts that target specific aspects or areas of their work. They'll start by typing a prompt into the chat window and then copying and pasting the portion of work for which they want feedback after their prompt. (You'll notice that I sometimes use *please* in my prompts. Politeness isn't necessary. It's just how I interact with others, even machines.)

By asking for specific examples and guidance, students can receive suggestions from ChatGPT that they can use to enhance their writing while maintaining their unique voice and style.

Questions to Ask ChatGPT

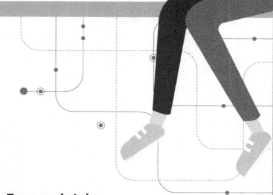

General feedback
Provide feedback on this using strengths and weaknesses.

Structure feedback
Can you review the structure of this essay I wrote on ____?

Grammar and punctuation
Please check the grammar and punctuation in this sentence or paragraph.

Clarity and coherence
Can you help me improve the clarity and coherence of this passage?

Ideas and content
Please give me feedback on the ideas and content in this paragraph or essay.

Vocabulary and word choice—
Can you suggest better word choices or more precise vocabulary for this sentence or paragraph?

Tone and style
Please review the tone and style of this piece of writing.

Formatting and citations
Can you check the formatting and citations in my paper?

Thesis statement and argument
Please evaluate my thesis statement and argument in this essay.

Suggestions for improvement
What are three specific ways I can improve this piece of writing?

Tailoring prompts to the area they want feedback on allows students to get targeted and actionable advice from ChatGPT to help them improve their writing.

For ideas and suggestions before and during the writing process
The following prompts can help students brainstorm, develop, or expand topic ideas as well as improve their vocabulary skills and writing techniques.

Thesis statement
What are some examples of strong thesis statements about [topic]?

Idea generation
Can you give me some examples of possible arguments for and against [topic]?

Topic sentences
Can you provide examples of compelling topic sentences for a paragraph discussing [topic]?

Vocabulary enhancement
Can you suggest some synonyms or more precise words for [a specific word]?

Transition phrases
What are some examples of transition phrases I can use to improve the flow of my essay?

Supporting evidence
What are some examples of evidence or data I can use to support my argument on [topic]?

Counterarguments
What are some potential counterarguments to my claim about [topic], and how can I address them?

Analogies and metaphors
Can you give me examples of analogies or metaphors I can use to explain [concept]?

Conclusions
What are some examples of effective concluding sentences for this paper that leave the reader thinking?

Paraphrasing
How can I paraphrase this idea without changing its meaning?

15 Ways to Infuse the Writing Process with AI Tools

1 **Brainstorming Sessions**—Use the power of LLMs to conjure up imaginative ideas, themes, or intriguing prompts that will inspire students to dive in and expand their writing adventures!

2 **Collaborative Storytelling**—Have students work together with AI models to create stories, with each person contributing a sentence or paragraph and the AI providing suggestions or alternatives.

3 **Vocabulary Expansion**—Encourage students to use AI models to discover new words or phrases to enrich their writing, fostering a broader vocabulary and more diverse language use.

4 **Research Assistance**—Teach students how to use AI tools to summarize articles or extract key information from large volumes of text, improving their research efficiency and comprehension.

5 **AI-assisted Editing**—Teach students how to use AI tools for proofreading, grammar checking, and improving the clarity of their writing, while emphasizing the importance of human judgment in the editing process.

6 **Opposing Viewpoints**—Use LLMs to generate arguments and counterarguments on specific topics, helping students build their critical thinking and persuasive writing skills.

7 **Creative Inspiration**—Use LLM-generated text as a starting point for poetry, short stories, or essays, challenging students to build upon the AI-generated content to create original works.

8 **Analyzing AI-generated Content**—Have students critically evaluate AI-generated text, identifying strengths, weaknesses, and potential biases, to build their critical reading and thinking skills.

9 **Exploring Writing Styles**—Encourage students to experiment with different writing styles, tones, or genres by using AI-generated examples as inspiration or templates.

Bonus:

- Student or Teacher Prompt Idea— I am interested in _____. What are 10 interesting ideas about _____ I could research?

- Word Bank Prompt——Can you give me a list of words that might make this paragraph better (insert paragraph)

- Feedback—Can you provide feedback in the form of strengths and weaknesses

- Rebuttal Prompt—Can you give me a rebuttal to these ideas (insert ideas)

- AI-Generated Outlines: AI can be used to generate outlines for writing assignments, providing students with a starting point for their writing and helping them to organize their thoughts more effectively.

 10 Sentence Expansion and Compression—Teach students how to use AI tools to expand simple sentences into more complex ones, or to condense lengthy sentences into shorter, more concise versions, improving their ability to write clearly and effectively.

 11 Journaling and Reflection—Encourage students to use AI tools to support their reflective writing or journaling practice, with the AI providing suggestions or prompts to help them explore their thoughts and emotions.

 12 AI-Assisted Role Play—Ask the language model to take the role of a historical figure, scientist, or professor to offer ideas about something.

 13 News Analysis—Task students with analyzing AI-generated summaries of news articles, focusing on identifying potential biases, accuracy, and the need for further research

 14 Inquiry Writing Project Ideas—Use AI-generated writing prompts to inspire students to explore new topics, perspectives, or genres in their writing assignments.

 15 Mentor Texts—Use AI-generated examples as mentor texts to help students understand the structure, organization, and characteristics of various types of writing, such as persuasive essays, narratives, or expository texts.

Writing is changing. Will our students be ready?

Writing is evolving. We can resist these changes and focus on ways to prevent students from cheating, but these concerns only anchor us to the past. Instead, as we embark on this shift in our perception of writing, let's consider the intricate aspects of the writing experience. Yes, writing still includes words, sentences, and paragraphs. It is imperative to our students' futures, however, that we look forward and explore how we can leverage AI to elicit even better words, sentences, paragraphs, and papers from our students.

We have a remarkable opportunity to provide each student with a writing assistant—a means to generate fresh ideas, check grammar, and ultimately improve their writing skills. No, AI-generated text isn't always perfect, but it offers a valuable starting point.

By teaching learners how to use these tools effectively, we can empower them to become better communicators. So, rather than suppressing this potential, let's embrace and celebrate it!

AI-Infused Strategies for Traditional Student Writing Assignments

Language teachers' hearts swell with pride as they watch students unravel the beauty of language. Educators across all grade levels love to see their learners' communication skills improve as they learn to craft enchanting narratives and express themselves effectively and eloquently.

AI writing tools have ushered in an era of unparalleled possibilities for educators who seek to revolutionize traditional writing tasks. With these new writing assistants come the potential to enhance students' writing abilities. In the previous chapter, we saw a few ways we can infuse AI into the writing process to empower students to improve their word choice skills, produce higher-quality work, and ultimately, develop a stronger command of the written word.

Note: AI tools and language models should always be used as supplements to, rather than replacements for, the guidance and instruction provided by teachers. By leveraging these technologies alongside traditional teaching methods, students can enhance their writing skills and produce higher-quality writing.

As an English teacher, that part is really exciting for me. I also am thrilled by the prospect and potential of blending old and new—of taking the best aspects of traditional writing assignments and infusing them with AI strategies that stretch learners' thinking skills, curiosity, and ability to communicate well. That's the focus of this chapter. Well, that and helping students learn how to ask for help from a tool, such as ChatGPT or Google Bard, rather than simply asking it to write the assignment for them.

We'll start with one of the most common writing assignments: the research paper.

The AI-Infused Research Paper

Traditional research papers are characterized by their structure and formality. Candidly, they are not typically the highlight of a student's classroom experience, although technology and a focus on student-led learning are changing that.

By encouraging students to pursue topics they are genuinely passionate about, for example, we improve the experience by making it personal. When we allow them the freedom to choose their focus, curiosity fosters a deeper engagement with the research process, which cultivates a more meaningful learning experience.

Access to information via the internet made it easier to give students agency and improve their efficacy in crafting research papers. Now, with LLM-powered tools, such as ChatGPT, we can further enhance the traditional assignment of writing informational and expository papers. By providing support and guidance throughout the writing process, AI tools equip students to sharpen their skills and give them a confidence boost.

Here are a few ways to infuse a research paper assignment with AI:

Topic Selection—AI tools can suggest a range of topics or specific questions to explore based on students' interests or assignment requirements. Up until now, coming up with an idea has been as hard for some students as finding research about their topics. I applaud this use of AI because it helps learners discover and select engaging and suitable subjects.

Research Assistance—LLMs can streamline the research process by recommending reputable sources for students to consult for their research. They can also identify possible bias and misinformation. Once students have selected a source, the tools can help them extract key information, facts, and statistics to support their arguments.

Organizing and Structuring—AI tools can guide students in creating clear and coherent outlines for their papers for proper organization and structure. For those who might need it, ChatGPT can offer tips on crafting introductions, organizing body paragraphs, and writing concise conclusions.

Vocabulary and Style—AI tools can provide students with suggestions for appropriate academic language, precise terminology, and clear phrasing to enhance the readability and effectiveness of their papers.

Editing and Revision—Students can get help identifying areas for improvement in their writing, such as unclear explanations or weak arguments. They can also ask for alternative word choices or sentence structuring to help them improve the quality of their papers.

Citation Assistance—AI can help students fact-check and validate sources as well as offer guidance on proper citation formats and styles, ensuring that students give credit to their sources and avoid plagiarism.

Feedback and Learning—Students can receive instant feedback on their writing, allowing them to learn and improve in real-time.

The AI-Infused Persuasive Writing Assignment

For the traditional persuasive paper, a teacher might give the students a prompt and task them with the assignment of researching and writing a paper that persuades the reader to think a certain way. The essay often includes a five-paragraph format. This structure may be effective in teaching students to develop organizational skills and understand the role of supporting arguments, but it is inauthentic and thus unsuitable for real-world communication.

Persuasive communication is a valuable skill, so let's have students practice it in a way that prepares them for real life. Instead of, or in addition to, the traditional five-paragraph paper, consider having students write persuasive social media posts or campaigns, persuasive emails, business and food reviews, product advertisements, or even comments on a social post.

You and your student can use AI models to enhance persuasive writing assignments and craft well-written and compelling content.

Here are a few ways to infuse a persuasive writing assignment with AI:

Idea Generation and Brainstorming—LLMs can help you and your students generate ideas and brainstorm potential topics for their persuasive assignments. Simply input an idea or topic of interest and ask your favorite language model to suggest specific persuasive topics, arguments, or campaigns. Then, ask the AI tool to provide examples of different perspectives on an issue. Exploring various viewpoints allows students to develop a well-rounded understanding of the topic.

Develop Stronger Arguments—AI can assist students in formulating persuasive arguments supported by evidence. Students can use AI to develop a clear and strong thesis statement that effectively conveys their main argument. They can ask for examples of evidence, statistics, or expert opinions that can support their arguments. AI tools can also make suggestions on how to create concise language for a product review or social media campaign.

Find Possible Counterarguments and Rebuttals—An essential aspect of persuasive writing is addressing counterarguments and providing rebuttals. By asking an LLM to identify potential counterarguments, students can discover what objections they will need to address and refute to reinforce the validity of their main argument.

Additional Writing Assistance and Editing—Students can ask the language model to review their writing. By considering the AI's suggestions, they can improve their sentence structures, expand word choice, and make ideas more compelling. They can also use AI to check for grammatical, spelling, and punctuation errors as they polish their final drafts.

Feedback and Revision—Students can cut and paste their persuasive paper into ChatGPT or a similar tool and request feedback on content, organization, and language use. They can then use that feedback to make changes during the revision process.

AI-Infused Narrative Assignments

Storytelling is another valuable skill for today's communicators. For a modern twist on a traditional narrative essay, consider making it a layered writing assignment (as discussed in the previous chapter) and using AI tools for support and guidance throughout the process. Creating a brand's story, an effective social post, or a mini-documentary (under three minutes), for example, encourages students to think beyond the page as they communicate their ideas.

Inspiration and Idea Generation—AI models can help students to get some inspiration for story ideas and even help them create more engaging story concepts, themes, or character ideas.

Organizing Thoughts—LLMs can help students structure their ideas by suggesting ways to outline their narrative by providing tips on creating a compelling beginning, a well-paced middle, and a satisfying conclusion.

Language and Vocabulary—An AI tool can help students improve their word choices and use of descriptive language. As an English teacher, however, I want my students to practice enhancing their writing with rich vocabulary, varied sentence structures, and engaging dialogue *before* turning to AI for ideas or suggestions.

Character Development and Dialogue—Use this new writing assistant to guide students in creating believable and relatable characters. They can ask it to provide suggestions on how to develop their characters' personalities, motivations, and backstories. Additionally, AI could be used to generate sample paragraphs, sentences, or dialogue to help students overcome writer's block, expand on their ideas, or refine their storytelling.

Editing and Revision—Students can get help in identifying areas that may need improvement or elaboration, such as plot inconsistencies, unclear descriptions, or awkward phrasing. AI tools can also provide suggestions for alternative word choices or sentence structures, helping students refine their narrative and improve overall readability.

Feedback and Learning—Students can receive instant feedback on their writing, allowing them to learn and improve in real-time. This iterative process can help them better understand the craft of storytelling and develop their skills as writers.

AI-Infused Descriptive Writing

I've noticed that students generally enjoy descriptive writing assignments. This type of writing allows them to unleash their creativity and bring their thoughts to life through the power of language. Harnessing the potential of AI tools can significantly enhance students' ability to produce rich, expressive, and vivid descriptive writing. Here's how:

Word Banks—Students can use AI tools to generate a list of descriptive words, phrases, and idiomatic expressions tailored to the subject they are describing. The word bank can then serve as a resource from which students can draw inspiration. With ideas to keep them going, they learn to enrich their writing and create a more immersive reading experience.

Feedback on Expressive Language: AI tools can provide real-time suggestions, enabling students to elevate their descriptive language, employ more captivating and evocative imagery, and incorporate richer sensory details into their writing. This support challenges students to convey their thoughts more effectively and engage their readers on a deeper level.

Targeted Feedback: Similar to the other examples, AI tools can offer personalized feedback and targeted improvements for each student. This feedback allows students to learn how to refine their writing skills and fosters a better understanding of descriptive techniques.

Using AI the *Right* Way for Writing

In this new frontier, AI-infused classrooms will use tools like ChatGPT to guide students through every stage of the writing process. These tools, remember, never replace the teacher. They are supplements and serve as ready writing and research assistants.

The key to harnessing the power of AI lies in teaching learners how to use it for inspiration and feedback. Idea generation and refinement, sourcing credible research, expanding vocabulary, and editing assistance are all invaluable applications of these incredible tools—for our students and us. When we use these tools in conjunction with good pedagogy, we can transform and expand the way students learn to write and communicate.

In this new frontier, AI-infused classrooms will use tools like ChatGPT to guide students through every stage of the writing process. These tools, remember, never replace the teacher. They are supplements and serve as ready writing and research assistants.

Writing-Process Assessments for the AI Infused Classroom

As a teacher, I've always believed in the power of reflection. I view it as a crucial part of the learning process. So when it came to assessing my students' writing, I decided to incorporate reflection throughout the writing process, not just at the end. The goal was to help them become more self-aware writers. Their reflections on their process became part of what I assessed, both along the way and with their final work.

Assessing the *process of writing* can provide a more comprehensive view of a student's writing abilities than assessing only the final product. Real-time and ongoing evaluation helps learners develop their skills because they can apply that feedback the right way. This is also true of regular reflection. When students pause to review their work, rather than rushing through the writing process, they can apply their insights and hone their skills. The grade book outcome of this practice of assessing the process of writing is often to attain higher scores, but the more valuable result is learning that sticks.

It's often said that students need to write more to be better writers; this is only partly true. The strategies I'll discuss in this chapter have taught me that writing improves when students have time and guidance for reflection and are inspired and encouraged to write what they are passionate about.

With the rise in the use of AI writing tools, ongoing assessment and reflection are more important than ever—for a few reasons. First, it requires students to think about their ideas more deeply, a practice that makes them better learners and better writers. It also makes them share their progress along the way. If your concern is that students will rely on AI to "do everything for them," requiring them to document their writing process from start to finish can help ensure their participation in every step. In this chapter, I'll share a few ways that I've used reflection as part of the writing process.

The Writing Process Journal

A writing process journal is a place for students to document their ideas and progress throughout a writing assignment. What's included? Everything! Students can reflect on each stage of the process: brainstorming, outlining, drafting, revising, and editing. They can share how they developed their ideas and made decisions about their writing.

Keeping a writing process journal is not complicated, but students have to be taught *how* to do it. Students can use sticky notes on a whiteboard like FigJam (figma.com/education) or even an actual old-school journal.

I'm going to be honest: Students don't always want to take the additional steps of documenting their work. It requires a thoughtful approach to writing—and sometimes they would just rather be done. But the purpose of any assignment isn't simply completing it; the goal is to ensure learning. And that's where the journal comes in. Here's how I use this tool with my students:

Setting Writing Goals

To cultivate a growth mindset in my students, I have them set writing goals for the academic year. For each assignment, they identify which of the goals they've set align with the specific type of writing they will be working on. Then, they select three targeted areas they want to refine within that piece, such as word choice, voice, or grammar. This approach empowers students to focus on improvement and take charge of their education by tailoring their learning experiences to fit their needs.

Learning from Feedback through Reflection

Because students might use AI to help them with assignments or, worst case scenario, do the assignments for them, we have to take a different approach to feedback, whether it comes from us, their peers, or the AI..

Even before ChatGPT came into our classroom, I knew that the way students interacted with feedback was important. The last thing I wanted was for students to get a grade on a paper but never look at my notes to them. If I allowed that to happen, offering constructive comments on their work was a waste of my time and, more tragically, the students would not learn how to improve their writing.

Determined to create an engaging and meaningful reflective- and process-based experience for my students, I made reflection part of the writing assignment. I knew it would push students to think more deeply about their work throughout the writing process.

When I began this process, students used sticky notes. I encouraged them to consider peer feedback as well as my feedback and then choose three comments or suggestions to reflect on. Writing on sticky notes, they asked questions about and evaluated each of the suggestions and the reasons behind the feedback. They also made notes about whether they agreed with the input. Finally, they made a note about the change they had made and why.

This self-evaluation process fostered a more comprehensive understanding of their writing development and promoted a constructive approach to receiving feedback. It was time intensive, for sure, but it made students think about their writing.

Today, the feedback they receive is also AI-generated. And they may choose to make their comments in a digital format rather than on sticky notes, but the process is the same and the reflection remains valuable.

Create New Assessments for Writing
Bridging the Gap from Doing to Showing

⭐ **Evaluate the Entire Process**

Shift to Student Led Growth: Let students use the success criteria to ask Chat GPT for the feedback - not the teacher.

Evaluate the collaborative process of peer review

Include a way for students to talk about their partnership with an LLM

Shift the emphasis of writing assessment towards critical thinking, argumentation, and analysis

⭐ **Evaluate the Synthesis of Written Information-** Include graphical elements like infographics to help students synthesize and show learning

Reflecting on Mentor Texts

Another means of encouraging reflection is through mentor texts. I set up digital mentor stations for students. Each one focuses on a specific area of writing development. (I could have gone old-school and printed out the mentor texts, but I wanted my students to have access to the mentor texts from home.)

For students who want to focus on improving word choice in their assignments, for example, I set up a digital station featuring mentor texts showcasing exceptional use of words. In the past, this has included materials such as the lyrics to Taylor Swift's songs like "Enchanted" and writings from authors they had been studying. Students visit these stations, explore the mentor texts, and then apply the insights they've gained to enhance their writing. The interactive approach provides examples of excellent word choice for them to emulate and inspires them to improve their writing.

For the grammar station, I gave them access to Grammarly and required that they make comments in their writing process journals on why and how they used this AI tool.

The first few times I used mentor texts in this way, I was happily surprised that many of my students took the reflection seriously and shared thoughtful insights on their writing processes. Some even identified areas they needed help with and suggested ways they could improve. I was impressed by their self-awareness and eagerness to learn.

So I took reflection a step further to really get into their process and thinking.

Enter Video Reflections on Process—A Two-Part Plan

Encouraged by the success of the written reflection, I introduced video reflections. I asked my students to create short videos, in Microsoft Flip, in which they would talk about their strengths and weaknesses as writers and share their thoughts on how they could improve.

We live in a world where ChatGPT can write assignments for students, but computers cannot replace or duplicate the video reflections that students create. Not only do these videos provide insight into students' thinking but they are an additional way to make sure they are doing the work and learning to write effectively.

PART ONE:
Talk about the Overall Content—Video One

Think of these videos as pseudo student conferences, which I'd ideally have with each student if time and class sizes allowed. While I may not always watch every video, they serve as valuable resources for students to reflect on their growth over time and provide a better understanding of their development throughout the year. The process encourages student agency and builds self-efficacy toward becoming better writers.

To create these videos, students capture screenshots of their papers and incorporate the images in their videos so that their face appears beside their paper on the screen. (Note: If grading the video for the process piece, it helps to keep the student's paper open next to the video so it is easier to read.) While discussing their progress, the students highlight specific sections of their work to provide a clear visual context for their reflections. They reflect on whether they met their goals or had room for improvement.

The videos provide a clear picture of each student's writing process and the challenges they faced. More importantly, it gives them insight into their journey as writers.

With the inevitable integration of AI into the writing process, fostering self-reflection becomes increasingly essential. By having students explain their writing choices and discuss the extent to which they utilized AI tools like ChatGPT, you can gain valuable insights into the impact of AI on their final work and hopefully ensure they maintain a healthy balance between technology and their creativity.

PART TWO:
Talk about What They Learned—Video Two

In a separate video, students reflect on their overall experience with the writing assignment and what they learned about themselves as writers. I've included ideas and sentence stems, but I've found that the more times students go through this reflection process, the less they rely on these prompts:

- During this assignment, I noticed that my writing improved in the following ways:
- One significant change I made to my first raft was ... and I was proud of it because ...
- I needed to make a change to my writing and this is what I did to accomplish that...
- The most valuable lesson I've learned in this unit was...
- My biggest strength in writing right now is...
- My biggest area of growth should be this going forward...
- I have grown as a writer during this assignment in these ways...
- One area where I still see room for improvement in my writing is...
- I used AI to help me write my paper in these ways...
- The paragraph I am most proud of is ...and here is why
- The idea I was trying to express was this...
- I think the best sentence I wrote was this ...

One of my favorite things about this reflection video is seeing how surprised students are by their growth and hearing what they've discovered about their writing process.

How AI Impacts the Reflection Process

With the increased use of AI in writing, the reflection process becomes even more important. As a teacher, I want my students to understand the role AI can play in writing and to critically reflect on their use of it. You may feel the same way.

With that in mind, make it clear to your students that AI tools are not substitutes for critical thinking and careful writing. Instead, encourage them to think of them as just that: *tools* that can help them refine their writing skills and identify areas for improvement.

To ensure that students are engaging in critical thinking while using AI, consider incorporating questions in the reflection process about how and why they used tools like ChatGPT, Grammarly, or others.

I have asked and will continue to ask students to reflect on how much they relied on AI to write their papers and to what extent they engaged in critical thinking and analysis during the process. I also ask them to reflect on how they used the feedback generated by the AI tools to revise and improve their writing. Because reflection is part of the writing assignment, I don't have to worry that they used AI exclusively. Hearing about their process in their words allows me to make adjustments in my teaching and will alert me of the need to head off the overuse of AI if it becomes a problem.

By encouraging students to reflect on their use of AI in the writing process, we can promote a deeper understanding of the role that technology can play in writing. The goal is for students to view AI as a tool that can complement, rather than replace, their critical thinking and creativity.

Incorporating reflection into the writing assessment process is a powerful way to help students become more self-aware writers, whether they are using AI tools or not. By reflecting on their writing process, peer feedback, the revision process, writing goals, and overall writing experience, students can gain valuable insights into their writing strengths and weaknesses and become more effective writers.

Documenting Learning in AI Classrooms

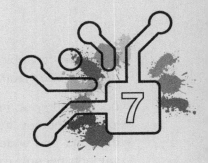

The Infused Classroom approach is about adapting education methods to support student learning in our rapidly changing, technology-driven world. Using only old methods, even those based on sound pedagogy, won't prepare today's students for their futures.

Forward-thinking teachers realized a while back that they needed to update what they taught, how they taught it, and why they were requiring students to learn it. In response to society's constant and almost unlimited access to information, one early and critical shift was to move away from having students read and regurgitate information and toward asking them *unGoogleable* questions—the kind of questions that make learners think, not just turn to their devices and search for the "right" answer.

Now, students don't only have access to information. AI tools will put the information together for them, providing the words they need and potentially fooling them into believing AI (or any other algorithm-driven platform) has all the answers. You and I know that's not true.

It has never been more important than it is today to empower our learners to engage in critical thinking. Our job is to push them to explore and evaluate concepts rather than simply consume information. Equally important, we must find ways to tap into their curiosity and imagination and draw out their ability to create.

It's another shift—one that can be difficult for teachers at times. Most of today's educators were not asked to learn and think this way as students. It's a new process for everyone, and it can be uncomfortable to try an approach that is so different and feels somewhat nebulous.

Enter the concept of **documenting learning**, a practice that harnesses the power of the creative process to foster a deeper understanding of learning. As Silvia Tolisano and Janet Hale explain in their book, *A Guide to Documenting Learning,* it provides "a visible, interconnected, meta-cognitive approach for creating evidence of one's learning process."[1]

Documenting learning refers to the process of capturing and reflecting on the learning journey. It provides a comprehensive record of a student's progress, thoughts, and understanding. The purpose of documenting learning is to help students become more self-aware, take ownership of their learning, and develop metacognitive skills. It allows learners to analyze their thought processes, identify areas of improvement, and set goals for future growth. Additionally, documenting learning enables educators to gain deeper insights into student progress, adapt instruction, and offer meaningful feedback. It also offers teachers a more profound and nuanced understanding of their journey toward proficiency.

Digital Tools for Documenting Learning

Documenting learning extends beyond simply asking students to explain their thinking in writing. Why? Because it requires students to think more deeply and create something original. It involves recording evidence of learning experiences, challenges, and growth using a variety of formats including written reflections, visuals, audio, video, or digital portfolios. In doing so, it counteracts the temptation to simply copy and paste AI-generated "thoughts."

While there are many digital tools available, the six options listed here are, in my opinion, the best choices for creating meaningful documentation of learning:

Microsoft Flip
flip.com

Canva for Edu
canva.com/edu

Adobe Express
express.adobe.com

Book Creator
app.bookcreator.com

FigJam
figma.com/education

Padlet
padlet.com

---

1   Silvia Tolisano and Janet Hale, *A Guide to Documenting Learning*, Thousand Oaks, CA: Corwin, 2018.

In Chapter 8, you'll find more information and specific strategies for using these tools. Before we get there, however, let's focus on how this process of documenting learning empowers students and equips us as educators to be more effective in our efforts to help them thrive in the world of AI.

Documenting Learning by Creating

Educators face the challenge of helping students move beyond superficial understanding to truly grasp complex concepts. One powerful approach to achieving this is by engaging students in the process of documenting their learning through creative expression. This not only fosters a deeper comprehension of the subject matter but also cultivates valuable skills such as critical thinking and problem-solving. By encouraging learners to create and reflect on their understanding, we can transform the classroom into a dynamic space where students take ownership of their learning journey and rise to the challenges of the twenty-first century.

Documenting learning requires students to synthesize their learning, identify essential components, and create a visual representation of their understanding. These visual components could include graphics, posters, infographics, videos, sketchnotes, and more.

To facilitate this process, teachers often place students in groups to brainstorm, using tools like mind maps or graphic organizers. This helps learners organize their thoughts and main ideas.

Once their thoughts are organized, students begin considering how to visually represent their learning. As they create, they engage more deeply with the information, synthesizing it in the process. Synthesis is a proven learning strategy that helps solidify understanding.

It's essential to note that merely completing a graphic organizer only involves students in recall exercises, which doesn't lead to deeper learning experiences. To achieve a more profound understanding, students need the opportunity to go beyond this to creating, thinking, summarizing, and justifying. These processes enable students to make connections, resulting in a comprehensive grasp of the subject matter. In other words, they experience deeper learning.

Neglecting this vital creation and synthesis step can lead to superficial learning, preventing the development of deeper comprehension.

Incorporating Video Reflections for Deeper Understanding

In a world of AI, where words can easily be accessed by students, teachers need to get better at assessing for thoughtful and essential understanding. Creating a visual representation, such as a poster or infographic, is only the first step.

The next step is documentation. In other words, we need to capture our students' thinking, their process, and their reflections. This can and should be done in writing, but we also need to, as author and educator Stephanie Harvey says, make thinking *audible* and *visible*.

This is where we need to have students press RECORD. In the previous chapter, I mentioned using Microsoft Flip for reflection videos for writing assignments. It's also an excellent tool for documenting other types of learning. It allows students to capture their thoughts in a creative and fun way. For example, you could have your students upload a graphic they've created to Microsoft Flip and then use the video feature to explain the *what*, *how*, and *why* behind their creation.

Why is incorporating a video reflection in our lesson essential now?

As one of my favorite educators, Tara Grandy from Oklahoma City, once said to me, "If a student can tell you what they have learned, chances are they have learned it." That is the primary reason to use video: It allows us to listen to students' thought processes and hear them explain what they've learned. Video is an effective medium for assessment that requires both critical and creative thinking.

The concept of **visible thinking** is at the core of documenting learning through video. By observing and listening to students' thoughts, we can address misconceptions and encourage them to articulate their learning. This approach also provides a genuine insight into their learning journey by ensuring that learners express their understanding using *their* words, rather than relying on AI-generated responses.

Moving toward Assessments Based on Critical Thinking

Documenting learning doesn't have to come at the end of a project. An advanced pedagogy practice is to have students record a pre-assessment video at the start of a unit and then continue to document their learning journey. At the end of the unit, students can compare their initial video with their final work and reflect on what they've learned along the way.

Here's how this might look in a science class beginning a unit on cells. Each student records a video of themselves discussing their existing knowledge about plant and animal cells. After engaging in learning activities, such as experiments, readings, and media-rich sources, the students create graphics that illustrate the inner workings of a cell. Next, students import their graphics into Microsoft Flip and conduct a mini-lesson explaining the details in their illustration. This integration allows them to showcase their newly acquired knowledge in their words.

Differentiation has never been easier!

Advanced Tip: While watching the pre-assessment video, the teacher might discover that some students already know about the inner workings of cells. In that case, students have the opportunity to delve deeper into the topic using additional resources the teacher quickly and easily gathered from ChatGPT.

Where the advanced pedagogy comes in is having students compare their initial video with the final mini-lesson, reflecting on their learning journey. They can discuss the most effective learning strategies, key takeaways, and any lingering questions.

Using video enables students to express their thoughts in their own words as they synthesize their learning experience. The mini-lesson as well as the reflection video at the end of the unit provides an authentic look at their growth, something that is valuable to the student as well as the teacher who can accurately assess each student's understanding of the topic.

Sharing Learning and Encouraging Collaboration

Learning—and videos—are meant to be shared! This is the next step toward deep learning.

Sticking with our science class example, students use Microsoft Flip to download QR codes for the mini-lessons they created. The teacher hangs their cell illustration with a QR code to that lesson on the classroom wall. Students then scan the QR code, watch their peers' mini-lessons, and offer feedback or comments. Additionally, next year's students can scan QR codes to see good examples before they begin the unit so they can see what they are expected to learn during this unit.

Using Other Visual Representations of Learning

Creating graphical representations of learning is a way for students to demonstrate their understanding. The previous example called for an illustration, but there are a variety of creative formats students can use to showcase their learning. Here are a few ideas:

Posters—Students can design posters that present key concepts, ideas, or information in an engaging and visually appealing manner.

Infographics—Students can create infographics that display complex information, data, or concepts in a clear and concise visual format.

Sketchnotes—Students can use sketchnotes to visually represent their thoughts, ideas, and learning through a combination of text, drawings, and diagrams.

Original Pictures of the Concept—Students can draw or create original images that depict the concept they've learned, helping them to process and remember the information.

Icon Summaries—Students can create summaries using icons or symbols to represent key concepts or ideas, making the information more visually engaging.

Here is an example from Adobe Express that I love.

Comic Books—With Book Creator, students can create comic books to tell a story or explain a concept using a combination of text, voice recordings, and illustrations.

Timelines—Students can design timelines that visually represent the chronological sequence of events or the development of a concept over time.

Spotify Playlists with Cover Art—Students can curate playlists related to a specific theme or concept and design custom cover art that visually represents the topic.

News Stories—Students can write news articles or reports that cover a specific topic or concept. I love using Microsoft Flip's Breaking News lens option for this because it lets students easily incorporate photographs or illustrations to enhance their stories.

Illustrations—Students can create detailed drawings or artwork that demonstrate their understanding of a concept.

Magazine Covers—Students can design magazine covers that visually convey the main theme or idea of their learning, using images, typography, and layout.

All of these strategies allow students to document their learning visually. Just remember that this kind of documentation represents only one aspect of the learning cycle. To complete the cycle, it's vital to have students reflect on the process, ideally with video so that their learning is visual and audible.

I encourage you to make reflection and the documentation of learning part of your teaching strategy. (If you are not comfortable using it for every unit, start with a goal of incorporating it into at least three units this year.) The prevalence of AI, I believe, will make this process more necessary as it ensures that students are participating in the work at a meaningful level and taps into their critical and creative thinking skills. You may decide to make it a regular part of your students' learning process.

How Creative Formats Reveal Thinking and Understanding

As AI technology advances, documenting learning using creative formats will become increasingly beneficial for teachers and, most importantly, for students. When students create original work—something that, as of now, AI cannot do for them—they engage with the content on a deeper level than they might if they simply wrote a paper (*especially* if they used ChatGPT to write that paper). Providing unique and varied ways for them to showcase their learning also makes the documentation process more effective and enjoyable.

It may sound like an extra step or even several extra steps. Read on to learn more about the benefits of documenting learning and how these creative formats reveal your students' thinking and demonstrate and deepen their understanding.

Visualization—Visualization enables students to get a better grasp of complex concepts by representing ideas simply. When students create visual representations of their learning, they engage with the material, breaking it down so that they can understand the main points and expand on the underlying meaning.

Synthesizing Information

When students create artifacts of their learning, they are actively synthesizing information. This process involves breaking down complex ideas into simpler components and reassembling them in a coherent and meaningful way. Synthesizing information helps students internalize the material for better recall and future use.

Sketching the Learning

Sketchnoting, also known as visual note-taking or graphic recording, is a creative method of capturing information and ideas using a combination of hand-drawn images, and text. Instead of relying solely on traditional text-based notes, sketchnoting incorporates more interesting visuals, such as diagrams, icons, arrows, and other symbols to represent information.

The process of sketchnoting helps to boost comprehension, retention, and recall by leveraging the brain's ability to process and remember visual information more effectively than text alone.

And of course, you can have students tell you more about their sketches by creating a video reflection about their notes. FigJam (figma.com) is a great tool for this.

Unveiling Student Thinking and Understanding

When students create something, they often reveal much more about what they learned than they do when the assignment consists simply of text on paper. Writing tasks are just that: tasks that students want to finish. But when they are asked to talk about their learning, we find out so much more about them.

Incorporating writing and audio or video components is even more effective as it gives you two different data points and allows for a more complete assessment of their learning.

Allowing for diverse forms of expression allows students to effectively demonstrate their newfound knowledge and showcase their understanding. This is especially beneficial for students with learning challenges, such as dyslexia, which makes producing words on a page difficult, even when they know the content. The process of documenting their learning journey also allows all students to identify areas of confusion and empowers them to address these issues independently.

These creative representations benefit the educator as well. By evaluating the original work students create, teachers can uncover and then address misconceptions. This transparent learning process also provides insights into students' progress. As a result, educators can offer targeted feedback for improvement, further enhancing the learning experience for each individual.

Making Thinking Audible and Visible

As we navigate the ever-changing landscape of education in this new era of AI, embracing innovative and accurate approaches for assessment is crucial. Creative components that demonstrate learning in audible and visible formats benefit both learners and their teachers.

By pressing RECORD and sharing their thoughts, students provide invaluable insights into their thinking. Through video, they can communicate their ideas, showcase their comprehension, and confirm their academic progress.

As AI continues to evolve, teachers who rely solely on writing tasks to assess learning may encounter challenges. Embracing this strategy of making thinking audible and visible (not just written) is likely to become an essential part of ensuring all students have the opportunity to flourish in the modern classroom.

Blended Learning Tools That Support an AI Infused Classroom

As we move further into the digital age, educators must develop the skills and knowledge required to effectively integrate technology in the classroom. Much of my career has been devoted to and focused on this very thing.

I write, talk, and teach about infusing education with different digital tools not simply because I enjoy technology myself, but because I've seen firsthand how tech tools can greatly enhance learning experiences. The right technology used in the right way can foster collaboration on a variety of levels, challenge students to engage in critical thinking, and draw out curiosity and creativity in both students and educators alike.

The effective use of digital tools makes learning exceptionally engaging. Here's how:

- Edtech can inspire students to interact with the content in meaningful and memorable ways.
- Digital tools enable students to process information in ways that make sense to them—in writing as well as in visually dynamic and audio formats.
- Using the creativity embedded in many digital tools, students confidently explore different and innovative ideas, in part because they enjoy the process.
- When educators use these tools well, they empower students to become active, responsible, and adaptable learners who are ready to face the challenges of the future.

To understand how to effectively infuse digital tools into lesson design, let's first define **digital pedagogy**. Digital pedagogy is the methodology and practice of teaching that considers how the intentional use of technology can augment student engagement, amplify student voice, and generate more meaningful learning experiences.

Exceptional pedagogy deserves to be combined with truly meaningful technology to empower students. Today, that technology includes the use of AI tools.

The six tools I'll discuss in this chapter will enable your students to create content, interact with information, and converse about their learning. Equally as important, these tools offer the advantage of requiring critical thinking and original work—something that is vital in a world where it is all too easy and tempting for students to over-rely on AI.

The first four tools we'll review, Microsoft Flip, Canva, Adobe Express, and FigJam, are free for educators. You and your administrators will need to consider each of these companies' thirteen-and-under policies.

Without an explanation about the tools, parents often assume that students will spend time on the screen instead of learning the way they learned. Engaging in conversations with parents about the impact these tools can have on their students' academic and future success eliminates any misconceptions.

> **Exceptional pedagogy deserves to be combined with truly meaningful technology to empower students. Today, that technology includes the use of AI tools.**

Tip: If your district hasn't already approved one of these tools, ask parents to sign permission slips. When I've done this in the past, I included a video explaining why I wanted to use these tools and how we would use them. This explanation helped parents understand that I wasn't simply asking for more screen time and that, instead, we would be using these tools as vital, creative components of their children's critical thinking and deep learning experience, and to help me better understand my learners.

Free Tools for Educators

Explain Your Thinking with Microsoft Flip
Flip.com

Microsoft Flip is a video program that allows students to answer questions and, more importantly, discuss their learning. If you have ever listened to my podcast with Matt Miller called *The Digital Learning Podcast*, you have undoubtedly heard me rave about my love for Microsoft Flip. I believe Microsoft Flip is the most revolutionary tool available to us as educators in a digital world.

The articulation of ideas and thoughts is a foundational skill for learners. For the majority of students, reading and writing proficiency come after they learn to express themselves orally. Microsoft Flip provides learners with the opportunity to hone those oral skills.

The relationship between oral language skills and reading and writing development has been well-established in research. While strong oral skills may not be an absolute requirement for all students, they often contribute to better reading and writing abilities. The development of oral language skills supports literacy skills by fostering vocabulary, grammar, and thought articulation skills.

Too often, this learning strategy gets overlooked in the classroom. That's unfortunate because having students discuss their learning could be one of the most powerful ways to transform our classrooms. The good news is that it is easy to incorporate this practice using digital tools.

Microsoft Flip isn't the only tool you could use for this purpose. Some teachers, for example, have students upload work they've completed to a tool like Google Slides. The students don't create a video, but they can show the teacher what they've learned and discuss it on a designated slide. That is an okay practice, but I prefer using Microsoft Flip for its ability to combine the students' work examples, their creativity, and a video of them talking about their work and what they've learned.

I am always searching for digital tools that I can leverage to 1) help me better understand my students and 2) empower them to convey their learning experience. In the Microsoft Flip video(s) they create, students practice articulating thinking as they share what they've learned. This allows me to hear them describe their learning process in their words. (See Chapters 6 and 7 for more on the value of documenting the learning process.)

To get started with Microsoft Flip, visit ai-infusedclassroom.com/flip for an intro video.

The screenshot below shows a student using Microsoft Flip to share her learning process as she shows something she created in Canva. It's one example of hundreds that I could share. Because we keep the videos short, I'm able to watch them and learn more about my students than I would be able to if we were limited to class-time conferences.

As I've stated in previous chapters, we must adapt our teaching and assessment practices to address the fact that AI exists in our world today. We need to hear our students talk not only about the work they are turning in but also about what they learned in the process of creating it. Using Microsoft Flip in this way helps us better understand how much our students are relying on AI, where their writing or other work needs improvements, what they comprehend, and what they're missing. Additionally, as students practice articulating their thoughts by talking about what they've learned, they are sharpening the oral communication skills that will help them build their literacy and writing skills.

Create and Show Learning with Canva
Canva.com

This creation tool is free for teachers and students if it meets your school's privacy and data requirements, so be sure to check your district policy. Visit **canva.com/education** and select Teachers. Then simply enter your school email address to automatically receive the pro version at no charge.

Once you've set up an educator account, you can invite students into your account so they can begin to create using Canva's incredible range of creation features.

Canva is a graphics program that allows students to design and edit a wide range of content. Here are just a few things they can create with Canva:

- Social media graphics
- Presentations
- Whiteboard for collaboration
- Graphic organizers
- Make digital posters
- Infographics
- Biography covers
- Book covers
- Spotify playlists covers
- Resumes and portfolios
- Mind-maps and diagrams
- Video content
- Photos and images
- Unique images using AI
- Animations
- Memes or original GIFs
- Illustrations
- Websites
- Timelines
- Storyboards
- Comic strips

Or this Manifest project that was created by eighth graders:

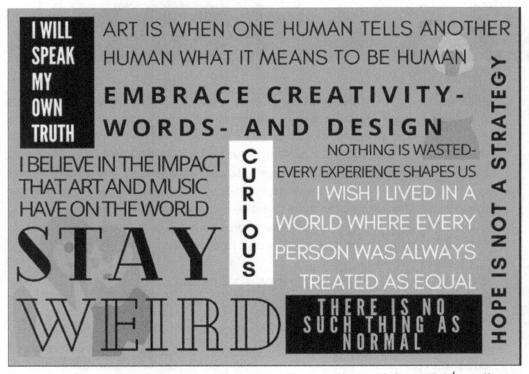

Check out the HyperDoc Manifesto Project at infused.link/manifesto.

In Chapter 4, I introduced the practice of layered writing assignments which call for students to create graphics to accompany their learning and writing experiences. Canva is perfect for this purpose.

As students interact with content and then convert their learning into original creations, the learning experience becomes constructivist, which increases the likelihood of it sticking. Anytime students engage in critical thinking and synthesize information, the information is processed at a deeper level.

Canva offers endless possibilities, so be sure to check out the AI-infused classroom learning series for an introduction to this tool. Access it by visiting infused.link/AIinfusedvideos.

By encouraging students to create artifacts (digital or tangible) that showcase their understanding, we can better assess their progress and adapt our teaching approaches accordingly. Engaging students in hands-on activities, collaborative projects, and creative problem-solving tasks allows them to develop crucial skills such as critical thinking, innovation, and effective communication.

By focusing on interactive learning experiences, we can ensure that students are equipped to thrive in an AI-infused landscape where creative skills are essential.

Create and Show Learning with Adobe Express
Adobe.com/express

Another one of my favorite digital tools is Adobe Express. Like Canva, Adobe Express is a graphics program, but its templates and webpage design features keep me coming back time and time again. The tool makes website creation a breeze, and the results are far superior to alternatives like Google Slides.

Using the templates, students can create "Pages" that serve as the final draft for writing assignments or classroom inquiry projects. The polished and professional feel of the work they turn in fosters pride in their creations. And as they use the website design tools to create a fully functioning site, the process of selecting images to represent their work encourages them to review and think more critically about their writing.

For links to Adobe Express challenges and to see their Page feature in use by a student, please visit ai-infusedclassroom.com for an intro video.

Interact with Information Collaboratively with FigJam
Figma.com

FigJam is the whiteboard tool we all hoped Google Jamboard would be. While Google Jamboard was helpful during the pandemic, it has seen few updates since and remains quite simplistic.

FigJam, on the other hand, offers a fun and interactive experience, complete with sticky notes, drawing capabilities, and emojis that allow students to engage with content. It's a must-use tool for every educator, and it's free for teachers and students.

The tool provides a great space for collaboration. Consider using it for any of the following activities:

- Brainstorming
- Diagramming
- Note-taking
- Sketchnoting
- Organizing ideas
- Having fun with stickers

The power of this tool is interaction. These collaborative environments encourage students to engage with their peers and share ideas. They can work together to solve problems, take notes, and interact with content—all of which are critical skills for thriving in an AI-driven world.

> To get started with FigJam, visit ai-infusedclassroom.com/figjam for an intro video.

Freemium Tools

Our next two tools have freemium versions, meaning you can access some of their features at no charge and have the option to upgrade for a fee.

The Creative Super-Power Book Creator
app.bookcreator.com

I am obsessed with Book Creator! With this versatile accessibility tool available, I often wonder why some teachers still opt for Google Slides. Maybe they just don't know about it yet. Let's change that!

Despite its name, Book Creator is not limited to book creation. The platform offers so much more, especially in the context of an AI-driven environment.

Yes, students can use Book Creator to transform their writing into illustrated, interactive books. They can also add voice narration, incorporate videos, use AI drawing tools, and even record themselves explaining their thought processes. Book Creator also has Canva integration, which means students can design in

Canva and add those elements to their book. This feature allows them to make professional-looking content that they are proud to share.

The versatility Book Creator offers enables students to create impressive projects, such as this water cycle project created by a third grader:

or this illustrated comprehension of *Pete the Cat* designed by a first grader. (This project also served as a fluency check for the teacher.)

Given its remarkable ability to enrich the educational experience for students, Book Creator should be an essential tool for every school district.

10 Creative Tools Book Creator Offers That Google Slides Doesn't

1 **Pen Tool** for drawing, illustrating, and annotating

2 **AutoDraw** makes drawing easier

3 **Record** your voice for narration and articulation of ideas

4 **Add Video** to include a variety of video content, not just YouTube or Drive

5 **Comic book** options

6 **Add 3D Models** (paid feature)

7 **Speech-to-text** typing

8 **Canva** integration

9 Various **Layout options**

10 **Templates**, such as newspapers, travel books, and many more

All of these features are in the app and do not require outside integration.
For an introduction to Book Creator, visit **ai-infusedclassroom.com**.

The free version of Book Creator comes with one library with forty books in it. Libraries and books can be archived at the end of the school year (or the end of a unit or project). When you archive books, you'll have access to up to forty more. You can restore or print your students' archived books, so you'll always have access to them. The paid-for version comes with 1000 books, unlimited libraries, and collaborative features.

How can you enhance the Book Creator experience with AI? Encourage students to generate exceptionally compelling content using the research and refining tools that AI offers. They can then harness Book Creator's versatile features to expand upon their ideas by incorporating illustrations, audio explanations, and other interactive elements that demonstrate their understanding of the subject matter. Using Book Creator in combination with AI amplifies the creative process and encourages deep engagement with the material.

Padlet for Metacognition
Padlet.com

I couldn't teach in today's world without Padlet. This digital tool provides a space for communication and collaboration between you and your students. The Padlets are like a virtual bulletin board with the power to post images, videos, information, questions, and answers.

Padlet's ease of use makes it my go-to choice for educators who are transitioning from tools like Google Slides to more impactful blended-learning experiences. Its simplicity and variety of uses make it an excellent starting point for teachers who are new to digital tools.

Although Padlet is a paid tool, you can get three free Padlets that can be replenished by archiving them. Because teachers often need more than three Padlets, however, I highly recommend districts invest in this tool.

Here are a few ways to use Padlet in your classroom:

Sharing resources—Teachers can use Padlet to compile and share resources related to a specific topic. Those resources (which you might choose to curate using AI) could include articles, videos, images, websites, and more. Students can access these resources as they complete assignments or prepare for exams.

Group projects—Padlet can facilitate collaboration among students working on group projects. They can use the platform to share resources, divide tasks, track progress, as well as provide feedback and support to one another.

Brainstorming—Create a Padlet board for students to share their ideas and thoughts on a specific topic or question. This encourages collaboration and helps generate a variety of perspectives.

Class discussions—Teachers and students can use Padlet to foster dynamic, interactive conversations by posting questions and responses for the entire class to view. This approach sparks further discussions and promotes critical thinking among students. Incorporating a Project Zero Thinking Routine, such as the See, Think, Wonder routine, enables students to learn from each other's perspectives and insights by observing their peers' responses on Padlet. It also allows you to see your students' thought processes. In other words, it makes their thinking visible.

Sharing Final Projects: With the platform's capability to add text, images, videos, and links to external resources, students can create multimedia-rich projects using Padlet. They can then share their work with their peers, giving them a bigger audience than just the teacher.

Bonus Tool: Wakelet

Wakelet.com

I couldn't stop with just six tools, so here's a bonus. Wakelet is a digital curation tool that is free for educators, and I'm a *big* fan. The platform allows teachers and students to collect, organize, and share various types of content from across the web. To do this you create a collection and simply add links to any relevant resource. This collection of resources can then be shared in a visually appealing and well-structured way.

Wakelet can enhance your students' learning experiences in a variety of ways. The interactive tool empowers them to improve their research, organization, and collaboration skills. Here are a few examples of how learners can use Wakelet:

Research Projects—Students streamline the research process by collecting and organizing resources in one place. With Wakelet, they have an easy way to share findings with their classmates or teachers. Additionally, you can have students use Wakelet to demonstrate their information validation skills by explaining the rationale behind citing specific sources in their papers. Merely citing a source is not enough; students need to understand and demonstrate the information validation process. I explain this concept in greater detail in *The Chromebook Infused Classroom* in the chapter titled "Information Literacy."

Digital portfolios—Students can create collections that showcase their work and process pieces into a digital portfolio.

Group projects—Wakelet's collaborative features allow students to work together on a shared collection. They can add content, comment, and organize resources collectively.

Study materials—Students can gather and share resources such as lecture notes, articles, videos, and other relevant materials to create a comprehensive "wake" for exam preparation.

These seven digital tools hold the potential to transform classrooms by fostering creativity and shifting the focus from traditional worksheet-driven instruction to interactive, hands-on experiences rooted in constructivism. By leveraging these tools, educators can revolutionize learning environments and empower students to actively engage in constructing knowledge and developing essential skills.

Questioning Mindset in an AI Infused Classroom

In an AI infused classroom, the power of asking questions takes center stage in shaping the future of education. As we embark on this exciting journey through the ever-evolving landscape of technology, the importance of cultivating a questioning mindset in students cannot be overstated.

This chapter delves into the vital role that questions play in nurturing critical thinking, fostering deeper understanding, and preparing students to navigate the complexities of an AI-driven world.

Have you ever been amazed by how relentlessly curious three- and four-year-olds can be? Witnessed the pure joy they derive from exploring? Envied their ability to absorb information like a sponge? Observed their tireless pursuit of knowledge as if they were flickering light bulbs? I've read that young children ask an astounding 300 questions a day on average, a number that plummets drastically once they reach the age of five. What happens during this developmental stage that stifles their unquenchable thirst for inquiry?

You guessed it. They start school.

And it's in our educational institutions where curiosity begins to fade.

That shouldn't be the case. And it doesn't have to be—*if* we are willing to learn how to use AI tools to keep the questions coming.

Children are naturally curious. With learning experiences shaped by AI, we can tap into that curiosity as we provide opportunities for them to explore, question, and grow.

Curiosity and AI

AI tools can act as catalysts for curiosity in the classroom. By infusing our teaching with these tools, we can nurture our students' innate sense of wonder. One way we can do this is by using AI to create personalized learning experiences that resonate with individual student's interests and abilities. When kids are pas-

Children are naturally curious. With learning experiences shaped by AI, we can tap into that curiosity as we provide opportunities for them to explore, question, and grow.

sionate or interested in a topic, they *want* to delve deeper into the subjects that captivate them. A tailored approach to learning instills a sense of wonder and excitement that permeates every aspect of their educational journey.

Modern classrooms have the potential to be more inspiring than ever before! Imagine the possibilities:

- ◉ Students are drawn into a world of exploration where learning becomes an exhilarating experience. Instead of squelching questions, school ignites their curiosity and drives them to unravel the mysteries of the subjects they study.
- ◉ Students access a wealth of information with a simple tap on their devices. This vast reservoir of knowledge—a staggering forty-five terabytes of information, which is equivalent to a half-million lifetimes— empowers them to explore the world like never before. The possibilities for learning are limitless!
- ◉ Students are encouraged to ask questions about anything that inspires them. Every new insight sparks their curiosity and drives them to investigate further.

Do the teaching and learning experiences in your classroom resemble those above? They can! We and our students have access to more information than ever before. Our job is to teach our students how to access and filter that information for bias and misinformation and then use it to reach new heights of discovery and understanding. By leveraging the remarkable synergy between human curiosity and AI-driven knowledge, we have the power to revolutionize the entire educational experience.

Reviving Curiosity in Education

Teachers are well-acquainted with the 4 Cs: critical thinking, collaboration, communication, and creativity. These are known as the pillars of successful learning, but did you notice that curiosity didn't make the cut? That omission concerns me because curiosity is the C that fosters lifelong achievement.

Consider the following questions:

- ◉ Does my classroom nurture curiosity?
- ◉ Do my students see value in asking questions?
- ◉ Or are they merely trying to meet my expectations for a grade?

If curiosity is lacking in your classroom (which is the case for many, if not most, of today's classrooms), I urge you to incorporate the following questioning strategies that draw on the power of AI. This essential C is a cornerstone of learning, one that students can build on for the rest of their lives.

Teach Students How to Ask Questions

When working with a tool like ChatGPT, asking the right questions makes all the difference in the quality of responses received. This makes question-asking skills vital—for our students *and* for us.

My favorite way to teach students to ask questions is using the Question Formulation Technique (QFT) from The Right Questions Institute (rightquestion.org). QFT is a six-step protocol developed to help students improve their question-asking skills.

Step One: Choose a Question Focus

The teacher presents Question Focus: a prompt, statement, or situation to serve as the basis for generating questions. The Question Focus should be clear, concise, and thought-provoking.

Here is an example that is accomplished using an image provocation:

Source: Right Question Institute

Step Two: Generate Questions

Students, working individually or in groups, brainstorm questions related to the Question Focus without discussing or debating the merit of the questions. They are encouraged to ask as many questions as possible, without worrying about the quality of the questions at this stage.

I set a time limit of five minutes for the brainstorming session.

Here are actual student questions from the Question Focus above:

1. Why is the 24 first?
2. What do the smiley faces mean?
3. Why are there three smiley faces?
4. How am I supposed to figure this out?
5. Is the answer 12?
6. Can I put any number for the smiley face?
7. Do three faces mean something?
8. Do the numbers have to be the same because the smiley faces are the same?

9. What numbers will work here?
10. Does it mean 24 is a really happy number?
11. Can we replace each smiley face with an 8?
12. Do any numbers work?
13. Can we do this for any number?
14. Does it always have to be smiley faces?
15. Do we always have to use three things?[1]

Step Three: Improve Questions

Students review their questions and determine whether they are open-ended or close-ended. They then discuss the value of each type of question and practice transforming questions from one type to another (*i.e.*, from open-ended to closed or vice versa).

Again, I set a five-minute time limit. Students don't need to work through every question.

Step Four: Prioritize Questions

Collaboratively or independently, students select the most important or compelling questions from their lists. They may use specific criteria provided by the facilitator to help guide their decision-making process.

I set a five-minute time limit on this step, as well, to keep students on task.

Step Five: Plan the Next Steps

Students, along with the facilitator, develop a plan for how they will use their prioritized questions to further their learning, research, or problem-solving.

Step Six: Reflect on the Learning

Finally, students reflect on the process and The Question Formulation technique they just went through. They make notes or comment on what they have learned about formulating questions and the value asking questions brings to their experience.

By following this six-step protocol, students can develop strong question-asking skills. As they sharpen these skills, their curiosity, critical thinking, and problem-solving skills grow as well.

---

1   Source: The Right Question Institute

Infusing QFT with AI

To infuse AI into the QFT process, you could start a unit with a provocation (Question Focus) that you discover using AI prompts. Or you could encourage students to come up with a general idea and then use ChatGPT or another LLM to refine or expand on their ideas to find a Question Focus.

We must equip learners to *ask* the right questions, not simply provide answers. They must be well-prepared to navigate and use this new wave of information, for both their betterment and that of the world. If we fail to prioritize curiosity as a fundamental element of learning, we will face the consequences that come with a lack of innovation and independent thinking.

Rather than telling students what they should know when they complete the unit, let them explore the topic by asking questions. Use the QFT process to spark curiosity and simultaneously teach them to ask good questions. Then allow students to **ask questions in a structured way with the help of AI.** This practice of asking questions can pique students' curiosity and interest in what they are about to learn. That interest and involvement in the exploration process help solidify learning in their minds.

As you begin the question-building process, conduct an assessment of each student's prior knowledge. Doing so will allow you to personalize their learning and ensure they stretch their capabilities and expand on what they already know. A pre-assessment also gives you a starting point for charting each learner's journey.

Today, AI can answer questions rapidly and even use questions to collate information for our students. This reality makes it all the more crucial for students to develop critical thinking skills. They must learn to ask thoughtful, meaningful questions as well as to evaluate and analyze the AI-generated information they receive—because not all of it will be accurate or unbiased. Questioning encourages students to identify gaps in their knowledge and seek more than surface-level answers. Furthermore, developing the ability to ask meaningful questions helps students become lifelong learners who are capable of adapting to the ever-changing landscape of AI and technology.

A great place to learn more about bringing the power of inquiry into your classroom is through books by Trevor MacKenzie, Kath Murdoch, and Jessica Vance.

Deep Learning and AI—
The Idea Engine for Teachers

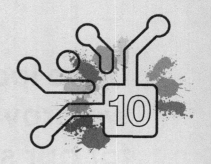

I opened this book with the questions teachers ask me every day about ChatGPT, one of the most common questions being, *Will we be able to detect ChatGPT responses for student cheating?*

Shoutout to @diannekrause for the Idea Engine idea!

Cheating. That's one of the first things that comes to most people's minds whenever this AI tool comes up in conversation.

Do you know what I *wish* people would think when they hear about ChatGPT?

Finally, the kind of learning we, as educators, strive to foster in all of our students: *deep learning.*

As educators, we want to create lessons that promote deep learning experiences for our students. ChatGPT offers us the ability to do that. But what exactly does this involve? And how can we combine this AI tool and exceptional pedagogy to create deep learning experiences in our classrooms? *Those* are better questions.

Most teachers will admit that worksheet packets do not provide the most engaging mode of learning. That said, they are readily available—easy to download or pull from a drawer. Given the numerous responsibilities laid on teachers' desks, calendars, and shoulders, it's no wonder that worksheets are too often the go-to solution. They're practical, fast, and easy to hand out and grade. They are not effective, though, for deep learning.

To foster deep learning, we must reimagine our approach to teaching and embrace innovative methods that encourage students to explore, collaborate, and make meaningful connections with the content.

Deep learning requires that we provide opportunities for our students to actively engage with information, synthesize it, and think critically about it, rather than passively consuming it in worksheet form. This is how we create dynamic and enriching learning experiences that prepare our students for the opportunities and challenges of the future.

Deep learning requires that we provide opportunities for our students to actively engage with information, synthesize it, and think critically about it, rather than passively consuming it in worksheet form. This is how we create dynamic and enriching learning experiences that prepare our students for the opportunities and challenges of the future.

In the past, assembling resources for deep learning experiences was often a daunting and time-intensive task. I recall a time when I had to purchase books at teaching supply stores and rely on resource packets that accompanied textbooks. Finding more interesting tools became a little easier when the internet came about. Websites offered ideas and educators could access time-saving resources from platforms like Teachers Pay Teachers.

Now, with ChatGPT, it's easier than ever before to offer students inquiry-based learning, problem-based learning, and deep learning experiences. Suddenly, every educator has access to a teaching resource assistant. Not to come up with quiz questions for us (although if you give it the right parameters, ChatGPT could help with that), but rather to provide a gamut of resources and ideas to foster deep learning. By leveraging ChatGPT's capabilities, we can create more engaging and more powerful learning than we could ever hope to with worksheets—and accessing those ideas is even faster and easier than running to the workroom to make copies.

What is deep learning?

Deep learning is a common topic of discussion in educational settings, but its true essence and practical applications in the classroom can be hard to picture and put into practice.

One barrier that prevents teachers from implementing deeper learning is the lack of clarity about what it is and how it is measured.

- Is it defined by the mastery of a subject?
- Does it imply a perfect score on an exam?
- Does it involve the ability to compose a well-reasoned and eloquent paper about the topic?

The answer is much more profound than these examples.

Jay McTighe and Harvey Silver offer this definition of deep learning in their book *Instructional Shifts to Support Deep Learning*: Deep learning is a "process through which an individual becomes capable of taking what was learned in one situation and applying it to a new situation."[1] More specifically, the authors contend, deep learning occurs when students come to understand and make sense of important ideas and processes *and* can transfer those understandings to new content and contexts.

What does this mean?

---

1 McTighe, Jay, and Harvey Silver. *Instructional Shifts to Support Deep Learning*. ASCD, 2018.

Here's a simple example of deep learning in a practical context: A student learns the concept of fractions in mathematics and later applies this understanding to real-life situations, such as dividing a pizza among friends. In this simple scenario, the student transfers a knowledge of fractions from the classroom context to a practical, everyday situation. By doing so, the student demonstrates the ability to apply learned concepts in different contexts.

Students applying what they learned to new or different situations seems easy, right? McTighe and Silver go on to state that "Researchers from Harvard University completed a six-year, in-depth study of 'successful' high schools throughout the United States. In their resulting book, *In Search of Deep Learning*, Jal Mehta and Lisa Fine reported that even in schools that have committed to deeper learning, the dominant mode of instruction involves teachers 'telling' students the content, with students 'bored and disengaged' rather than actively processing what they're learning."[2]

To achieve deep learning of content, which ultimately leads to the successful transfer of knowledge, we must not only provide students with the necessary information but also employ pedagogical strategies that actively engage them in constructing that knowledge base. Constructivism in education emphasizes the importance of students constructing their own understanding of the material through exploration, collaboration, and reflection. By adopting a constructivist approach, we can guide students toward a more profound grasp of the content, allowing them to make meaningful connections and apply their learning to real-world situations.

Additionally, it's necessary to remember that deeper learning occurs when we focus on big ideas rather than trying to hit every single standard. McTighe and Silver explain, "When it comes to addressing the issue of content overload, we agree with curriculum experts who recommend that educators should move away from trying to cover excessive factual material, and instead orient their curriculum around a smaller number of conceptually larger, transferable ideas."[3]

What else do we need for deep learning?

Educator and education researcher Elliot Sief noted in the post "What is Deep Learning? Who are the Deep Learning Teachers?" on the ASCD website that "Deep learning promotes the qualities children need for success by building complex understanding and meaning rather than focusing on the learning of superficial knowledge that can today be gleaned through search engines (and now Chat

---

2   McTighe and Silver's *Instructional Shifts to Support Deep Learning* referencing Mehta, Jal, and Sarah Fine. *In Search of Deeper Learning: The Quest to Remake the American High School*. Harvard University Press, 2019.

3   McTighe, Jay, and Harvey Silver. *Instructional Shifts to Support Deep Learning*. ASCD, 2018.

GPT and other AI). Deep learning instruction provides students with the advanced skills necessary to deal with a world in which good jobs are becoming more cognitively demanding. It prepares them to be curious, continuous, independent learners as well as thoughtful, productive, active citizens in a democratic society."[4] Sief made this observation in 2018, and it is even more true today with the prevalence of AI.

Deep learning principles provide the framework for teaching in a world where information is so readily available. Deep learning means...

- ⊚ Classrooms must be driven by fundamental, open-ended questions.
- ⊚ Those essential questions should lead to enduring understanding.
- ⊚ Learning allows for the construction of knowledge through thoughtful activities and interactions with the content.
- ⊚ Students continue to engage with the material until they can effectively talk about and transfer their learning to different applications.
- ⊚ Students know how to apply the knowledge and meaning they've acquired to real-world situations or cumulative classroom activities.

That final step is called "transfer of knowledge" and is the process that helps make learning stick.

The good news is that AI simplifies what was once a time-consuming task. Using ChatGPT, teachers can easily find essential questions as well as resources that students can use to access the content on their own.

Deep Learning in Action

How can AI help us foster deep learning in our classrooms? The following example outlines a process you could adapt to suit your subject level and students' needs.

Follow along! Open ChatGPT and enter the prompts I provide to see what responses you get.[5]

For this example, we'll design a learning experience for a fifth-grade American History class studying the Revolutionary War.

---

4   Sief, Elliot. "What is Deep Learning? Who are the Deep Learning Teachers?" ASCD In Service Blog, October 15, 2018, http://inservice.ascd.org/what-is-deep-learning-who-are-the-deep -learning-teachers.
5   I am using the ChatGPT 4 for this example. Who knows? Someday soon you might be using a more advanced version!

Start with an AI Query

Use this example to think about how you might do this in your classroom

Use this prompt: *Provide a step-by-step summary of the Revolutionary War for a 5th grade audience studying American history.*

Here is how ChatGPT 4 responded in May 2023.

> The American Revolutionary War, also known as the American War of Independence, was fought between 1775 and 1783.
>
> Background (1760s): The British government began to tax the American colonies to help pay for the costs of the French and Indian War. The colonists didn't like this because they didn't have any representation in the British Parliament.
>
> Growing Tensions (1765-1774): The colonists protested against the taxes with actions like the Boston Tea Party, where they dumped British tea into the harbor. This led to more tension between the colonists and the British government.
>
> First Shots (April 19, 1775): The war began when British troops tried to seize weapons from the colonists in Lexington and Concord, Massachusetts. The colonists fought back, and the Revolutionary War began.
>
> Declaration of Independence (July 4, 1776): The Continental Congress, a group of representatives from the colonies, declared independence from Britain. Thomas Jefferson wrote the Declaration of Independence, which explained why the colonists wanted to be free.
>
> Key Battles (1775-1781): Some important battles during the war included the Battle of Saratoga, which was a turning point in the war because it convinced France to support the colonists, and the Battle of Yorktown, where the British General Cornwallis surrendered, effectively ending the war.
>
> Foreign Support (1778-1783): The colonists received help from countries like France, Spain, and the Netherlands. This assistance was crucial in providing the colonists with military supplies, financial aid, and troops.

End of the War (September 3, 1783): The Treaty of Paris was signed, officially ending the war. Britain recognized the independence of the United States, and the new country's borders were established.

Aftermath (1780s): The United States formed a new government under the Articles of Confederation and later, the Constitution. The Revolutionary War had a significant impact on the world, as it inspired other countries to fight for their own independence.

Evaluate Knowledge and Pique Curiosity

Cut and paste the ChatGPT findings into a document and pass it out via Google Classroom, Microsoft Teams, or whatever classroom learning management system (LMS) you use.

1. Put students into groups of three to read and discuss the information provided.

2. Helping your learners identify what they know and where they have gaps in understanding is an important pedagogical practice, so once they've reviewed the material, have each student create a mind map or sketchnote to serve as an assessment of background knowledge.

    ⦿ During the activity, for example, students could circle or list vocabulary terms they don't know.
    ⦿ You or your students can add these terms to a class list that hangs on the wall or is posted on an online whiteboard.
    ⦿ You could highlight specific terms that you want to be sure students learn as they move forward in the study of content.

3. Tap into students' curiosity by having them work in their groups, this time as inquirers. Ask each group to come up with ten questions about the subject using the QFT protocol outlined in Chapter 9.

 OFFLINE TOOLS: Large piece of chart paper and colored pens

 DIGITAL TOOLS: FigJam Online Collaborative Whiteboard or Book Creator for the mind maps and sketchnotes; Padlet to compile the questions.

Extend the learning by having students interact with the content and notate their lists, mind maps, or sketchnote as they acquire new information or understanding.

 OFFLINE TOOLS: Give your students sticky notes and have them keep their mind maps or sketchnotes available in physical form. If they created them using a digital tool, print them so they can use sticky notes to interact with the content.

 DIGITAL TOOLS: Have students use sticky notes in FigJam or Book Creator to make comments on their observations. Vote on your favorite three and use comments to answer them as we progress. Think of it as an online anchor chart.

Why This Works

When you start the unit by having the groups read and review the AI-generated summary, students get a big-picture view before they dive into the content. By interacting with the material, creating mind maps and sketchnotes, and identifying what they're already familiar with and what they don't know or understand, they put themselves at the center of a constructivist learning experience. That student-led learning continues as they work in groups to come up with questions they have about the content.

Go Deeper

Foster discussion by creating a word cloud together. Ask each student to choose one word or phrase that comes to mind after seeing the timeline. Once all the words are on screen, you can use the word cloud to prompt deeper discussion about revolution as a whole.

 DIGITAL TOOLS: AnswerGarden or Curipod (Head to ai-infusedclassroom.com for more information on creating word clouds with your students.)

Provide activities that allow students to dig even deeper into the learning. Use various mediums to help students unpack the big ideas of the unit to allow them to see different ideas and aspects of the Revolutionary War:

- songs (period pieces or relevant songs from *Hamilton*)
- graphs
- stats
- links to resources
- videos
- additional text
- visuals from the period

You could also use ChatGPT to provide content from both British and American points of view. Ask them to consider both perspectives, looking for different narratives and possible biases. Then have them compare and contrast each side's version. Encourage students to engage in discussions, ask questions, and explore the Revolutionary War from various perspectives.

To show deeper learning, have students participate in a debate or discussion on the long-term consequences of the Revolutionary War and its relevance to current issues and events.

 DIGITAL TOOLS: Explore Board (Head to ai-infusedclassroom. com for more information on this idea.)

Synthesize Ideas and Demonstrate Learning

Synthesizing information is not about creating a product. We don't want a Revolutionary War poster made in Canva here; we want kids to sift through ideas and think deeply about what happened.

1. Encourage students to go back to their original sketchnotes, mind maps, questions, and sticky notes to review what they've learned.

2. Give students choices in how they show learning.

Here are two quick ideas that would allow students to synthesize and demonstrate deep learning:

Analyzing Decision-Making: *Discuss the difficult decisions made by key figures during the Revolutionary War and how they navigated the complexities of the conflict.* Students could create a video or podcast in which they speak as though they were alive during the war. Are they loyalists or patriots? What swayed them to choose one side over another? In a second video or podcast, have them talk about how what they learned applies to the idea of patriotism today.

 DIGITAL TOOLS: Microsoft Flip

 AI-INFUSED: Use ChatGPT to compile a list of some of the difficult decisions made by people during this time. Have students pick the one they think is the most compelling and explain why in detail.

Understanding the impact of taxation: *Use the issue of taxation without representation to explore the fact that Washington, D.C., has no representation in the federal government and how that must make its citizens feel.* Students could create a multimedia document or FlipTok (a short, TikTok-style video) that explains the various ways that the residents of Washington, D.C., are affected by not having federal representation. They could take a survey and use student responses to create a visual document or video highlighting three reasons Washington, D.C., should or should not have representation.

 DIGITAL TOOLS: Book Creator, Microsoft Flip, Padlet

 AI-INFUSED: Ask ChatGPT to explain in more detail why Washington, D.C., has no representation. Then ask the tool to list reasons why it should or should not have representation. Also, ask it to give you a rebuttal argument so students can sift through various points of view.

With the EASY button of AI, the possibilities to create deep learning opportunities for your students are nearly endless! Tools like ChatGPT make research and finding resources simpler than ever. And when you combine the time-saving features of AI with the power of digital tools, both you and your students can create activities, videos, audios, and multimedia materials that were simply too time-consuming to complete during class time even a few years ago.

You can see from this simple example that AI has the potential to transform the way we design opportunities for deeper learning in our classrooms. By harnessing the capabilities of AI tools, we can essentially multiply effectiveness as we tailor learning experiences to individual student needs—and we can save precious time in the process.

> **Teaching Tip:** AI can find relevant videos on specific topics. Try a prompt such as *Find 10 videos that would help 5th graders understand The Revolutionary War.* The quality of the results may surprise you. Of course, you'll want to verify that the videos listed are appropriate for your students and the unit's focus.

In their book, *Teaching for Deeper Learning: Tools to Engage Students in Meaning Making*, Jay McTighe and Harvey Silver promote the idea that students can actively participate in learning and interact with information by using seven thinking skills:

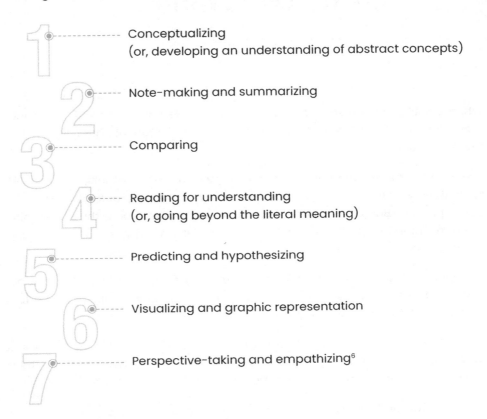

1 — Conceptualizing
(or, developing an understanding of abstract concepts)

2 — Note-making and summarizing

3 — Comparing

4 — Reading for understanding
(or, going beyond the literal meaning)

5 — Predicting and hypothesizing

6 — Visualizing and graphic representation

7 — Perspective-taking and empathizing[6]

When used properly, AI is a tool that allows students to evaluate information in different ways as well as practice their critical thinking skills. By employing these methods for demonstrating learning, we will be able to see their growth as they learn to ask the right questions to access and consider information.

AI is not a replacement for the human touch but a complementary resource we can use to enhance our teaching strategies and help us create more engaging and meaningful learning experiences. When we use AI to support deeper learning, we are empowering our students to thrive in a world where adaptability, problem-solving, and innovation are essential for future success.

---

6   McTighe, Jay, and Harvey F. Silver. *Teaching for Deeper Learning: Tools to Engage Students in Meaning Making*. Alexandria, VA: ASCD, 2019.

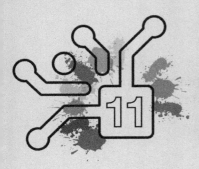

A Word about Plagiarism from Matt Miller

When ChatGPT was released and everyone was learning about AI assistants, a common cry sounded from teachers everywhere: "Students are going to use these to cheat!"

The truth is that, yes, students can (and likely will) use AI assistants, like ChatGPT, to do their work for them. Some will use it to avoid the work of thinking and skill development. (But let's be honest: Students have been doing the same thing using the internet, Spark Notes, or by copying their classmates' work for ages. AI just opens a new chapter.)

Using AI assistants, however, doesn't necessarily mean that students are not thinking. There's nuance here, and I've created a graphic to illustrate the fact that using AI doesn't always equal cheating.

Notice that the top of the spectrum is AI-generated—work done by AI alone. It ranges down to human-generated—work done only by humans. Let's think through this graphic together to consider what's cheating and what's not.

- ◉ Start at the top of the graphic: *Students copying and pasting responses from AI without any work or thinking on their own.* I think we can all agree that's not what we want.
- ◉ Go to the bottom of the graphic: *Without consulting AI or the internet.* That doesn't sound reflective of the world where they'll live and work in the future. That's not what we want either.
- ◉ Let's examine the nuance in the middle. With all four of these, the student is thinking as well as developing and demonstrating research, reading, and writing skills on some level, admittedly with some offering less rigorous practice than others. This is where the discussion gets tricky. And it's here you have to ask yourself, "Do I consider this cheating?" Of course, your answer may vary based on assignment, student needs, the subject, etc.

Rethinking "plagiarism" and "cheating"

AI-generated

Student plugged prompt into AI, copied response and submitted it to teacher.

AI created a response. Student read, edited, adjusted, and submitted.

Student created multiple AI responses, used the best parts, edited, and submitted.

Student wrote main ideas. AI generated a draft and offered feedback to improve.

Student consulted internet/AI for ideas, then wrote and submitted.

Student wrote all assignment content without consulting AI or the internet.

Human-generated

Key questions to consider:

? Which of these would you consider "cheating"?

? Which of these is relevant to our students' future?

? Which of these would you use in your work as an adult?

Graphic by Matt Miller (@jmattmiller) DitchThatTextbook.com  **DITCH THAT TEXTBOOK**

As you see in the *messy middle* of this graphic, the answer isn't as clear and obvious as saying "using AI to learn is cheating." As with any tech tool in the classroom, we must decide what's best for our students to help them learn and grow and prepare for the future.

As you consider how AI fits into your classroom, I encourage you to ask yourself the questions at the bottom of the graphic. We really do want to prepare students for the realities of their future, and AI will certainly be a part of it. Sit with that final question and get really honest about why you might want students to use AI in a lesser capacity than you use it now in your work as an adult.

Over time, I think the definitions of *cheating* and *plagiarism* will slowly change as artificial intelligence becomes more and more mainstream. We will see its common use in our everyday lives and in our work lives, and it'll become clear what's appropriate and productive in the classroom.

We don't want to end up on the wrong side of history. In the future, when we look back at how we handled this moment, we want to say that our students benefited from our forward-thinking approach in adapting to artificial intelligence. We want to prepare them for *their* future, not for the status quo of today.

Expanding Digital Literacies for an AI Infused Classroom

Before 2022, we needed to learn not to "trust everything we see on the Internet". In the future, we must learn "not to trust anything, unless proven real".

—Misch Strotz, CEO of Neon Internet

Imagine this: You've been an avid fan of Taylor Swift. You watched and rewatched videos of her concerts. When you finally went to a concert in person, you posted about it on social media, making your connection to Taylor Swift part of the vast, intricate world of data that many of us don't quite understand.

A few months after the concert, you come across a video of Taylor Swift talking—but something's off. You know she holds certain beliefs strongly, but this video conveys a different message. You watch it again. It's undoubtedly Taylor Swift, but she's advocating for a political candidate you know she wouldn't support.

You're shocked and horrified all at the same time. You wonder, *What just happened?*

The video appears in the same social media feed where you posted pictures of her concert. Is there a connection?

Having studied AI, you're aware that this could very well be a fake video designed to deceive you into believing that your favorite celebrity supports something she actually opposes. You suspect that someone created that video using AI and is targeting Taylor Swift's fans and followers with it. And now you're seeing it because the images you posted and all the concert videos you've watched have created a digital connection between you and Taylor Swift.

You only know the video is fake because you have studied AI in school and know this is something called AI-Generated Content.

What is AI-Generated Content?

AI-Generated Content (AIGC) refers to content or material created by AI systems. The content can range from being entirely accurate to potentially deceptive. In more concerning scenarios, content may be specifically designed to exploit a person's inclinations and potentially manipulate their understanding of reality.

Because AIGC can allow someone to create content quickly, it will allow people to get their messages to the masses in record time. Some of those people will be working for good purposes; others, unfortunately for society, will be working with destruction or personal gain in mind.

While the simplicity and speed of creating AIGC can be helpful for companies and creators, its use could have a darker side. The ease with which AI can make complex and realistic images and videos has given rise to deep fakes.

You've probably seen them in your social media feed already. **Deep fakes** are digital likenesses (photos, videos, and audio) of people that appear all too real—but they aren't. The manipulated data is used to target unsuspecting people with falsified stories. People have been creating fake images with Photoshop and similar programs for decades. But that was before AI.

With AIGC, the art of crafting deceptive stories, videos, and images has gained a formidable ally, which means that, at some level, all information should be viewed with a hint of skepticism. The truth is, just about any type of content can be manipulated and misused:

Text generation—AI models can generate human-like text based on a given prompt or context. This can be used for writing articles, blog posts, and anything meant to target people that might be more open to a particular slant on things. It is already happening in online media today.

Image generation—AI models like DALL-E and Firefly can generate original images based on text descriptions or prompts. This could allow for images that tell a story that is not true.

Audio generation—AI algorithms can generate music, sound effects, or even voiceovers, often using deep learning techniques like Generative Adversarial Networks (GANs). These AI tools can mimic people's voices to create deceptive and fake content.

Video generation—AI systems can generate video content, either by synthesizing new frames from existing footage or creating entirely new scenes using advanced computer graphics techniques.

While there are benefits to AIGC, we and our students need to be aware that not everything that appears and sounds real actually is.

Teaching students to consume and share information responsibly is an essential part of teaching in this rapidly evolving digital landscape. By helping students to recognize possible AIGC and even learn how to create some on their own, we empower them to discern fact from fiction and to look at content with a critical eye.

So, how do we help students understand AI and AIGC?

AI Literacies

You've heard of reading and writing literacy, financial literacy, cultural literacy, and digital literacy. And if you've developed literacy skills in these four areas it means you possess the ability to both comprehend relevant concepts and communicate your ideas effectively.

Acknowledging the need for a new kind of literacy—AI literacy—researchers at the University of Hong Kong conducted an exploratory review to evaluate what basic knowledge and skills are essential regarding AI. In their report, they propose four aspects of AI literacy education based on an adaptation of classic literacies: knowing and understanding, using and applying, evaluating and creating, and higher-order thinking activities.[1]

Knowing and Understanding AI—Teachers and students should be familiar with basic AI concepts, techniques, and their origins, such as machine learning, deep learning, and neural networks.

Using and Applying AI —Both teachers and students should be able to appreciate practical applications of AI, such as speech recognition and robotics, and understand how to train, validate, and test AI models.

Evaluating and Creating AI—This includes developing a deeper understanding of AI, applying one's learned skills and knowledge of analyzing, evaluating, and creating with AI to using (or even building) AI applications and algorithms to address practical needs and solve problems.

AI Ethics with Higher-Order Thinking Activities—Teachers and students should learn how to critically evaluate AI technologies for ethical and safety concerns associated with these applications in real-world situations. Knowing how to spot biases, misinformation, and even hard-to-detect coded bias is essential.

---

1   Davy Tsz Kit Ng, Jac Ka Lok Leung, Samuel Kai Wah Chu, Maggie Shen Qiao. "Conceptualizing AI literacy: An exploratory review." *Computers and Education: Artificial Intelligence,* Volume 2, 2021. https://doi.org/10.1016/j.caeai.2021.100041.

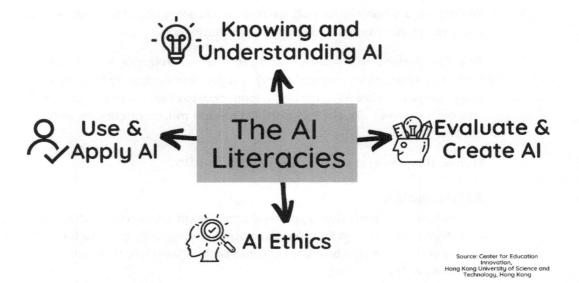

Source: Center for Education Innovation, Hong Kong University of Science and Technology, Hong Kong

What AI Literacies ChatGPT Recommends

In schools that currently offer any sort of AI literacy study, the focus is on lower-level thinking activities, such as knowing and understanding AI concepts and using AI ethically. That's a good place to start for younger students; however, as students advance in their education, it's essential to engage them in higher-order thinking activities. They need to learn not only how to use AI but also how to make informed decisions to use and create AI technologies.

After reviewing the study, I wondered whether those four literacies were enough to ensure we are all equipped for this world of AI. So I asked ChatGPT to offer its recommendations. Its suggestions were quite good. Some facets mentioned are included in the four literacies described by the study. I would argue that these additional competencies should be considered as we move forward.

Basic Understanding of AI—As a teacher, it's essential to have a foundational knowledge of AI concepts, technologies, and the core principles that drive them, including machine learning, natural language processing, and neural networks. This understanding will enable you to effectively teach and guide students in exploring the world of AI.

Critical Thinking and Evaluation—As educators, we must equip our students with the skills to analyze AI-generated content, outputs, or suggestions. This involves teaching them to understand potential biases, inaccuracies, or ethical issues, making sure they approach such content with a discerning mindset and make informed decisions.

LLMs draw from sources all over the internet, which means they can and do learn from and collate data that may include biases. Some of those may be negative or harmful or simply incorrect. Just as we teach students to evaluate a source's credibility, we and our students must learn to spot biases even in short fun interactions with the technology.

Data Literacy—As an educator, it's crucial to help students understand the significance of data in AI systems. It is important to recognize the value of data privacy and security, even teaching students about responsible data handling and the implications of AI in their lives.

Digital Communication—Teachers and students need to be taught how to effectively communicate with AI systems, understand how to provide clear prompts, and then interpret the output or refine that output using additional inputs or questions.

AI in Decision-making—Both teachers and students understand the value and limitations of AI, how it makes decisions, when to trust or question AI recommendations, and when human intervention is necessary.

Responsible AI Use: Students need to be taught the importance of using AI technologies ethically and responsibly, considering potential negative consequences, and taking steps to mitigate them.

AI Creativity and Collaboration—Learning how to leverage AI tools to enhance creative thinking, problem-solving, and collaborative work, both individually and within teams, is a must!

Maintaining a Growth Mindset Regarding AI

As we venture into the realm of artificial intelligence in education, we must adopt a growth mindset. We need to view AI as an opportunity for learning and skill enhancement, rather than seeing it as a menace to traditional methods or a gateway for student dishonesty and cheating.

This mindset is about adapting to change.

Adapting to change requires us to pause, consider our thoughts, and reassess our perspectives. By embracing AI as a means to propel learning, we will discover creative ways to integrate this technology into our teaching and learning experiences. With the right mindset, we can pave the way to creating innovative and inspiring classroom environments—the kinds of classrooms that make deep learning the norm for our students.

The Critical Role of Information Literacy in an AI-Powered World

Young people typically engage with technology through exploration and trial-and-error, rarely referring to manuals or waiting for instruction. This intuitive approach might work for some tasks, but simply hoping that students will naturally develop AI literacy skills is not an effective strategy—and it may even be a dangerous one.

As students interact with AI systems more frequently, they often do so without critically assessing the information they find—or even realizing the content was AI-generated. If they take what they see online or even the content generated by their own ChatGPT queries at face value, they are at risk of being misled.

AI grants us and our impressionable learners unparalleled access to vast amounts of data. In Chapter 2, I explained that AI models, like GPT-4, are trained by processing data from a wide range of internet sources, including blog posts, websites, books, research, and more. Much of that data is accurate and reliable, but some of it isn't; in fact, some of it is 100 percent false. The varied quality of an LLM's training data could potentially introduce biases or result in AI-generated information being based on opinions instead of well-researched facts. In light of this, we must teach students how to evaluate the validity, trustworthiness, and biases of AI-generated information.

In today's world, AI and information literacy are as crucial to success as reading and math skills. Students need to know how to discern truth from fake news and misinformation, and they aren't going to learn these essential skills by chance. If schools neglect the responsibility to teach students to master essential AI literacy skills, the outcome could be a new digital divide—one that separates those who can think critically about information and those who cannot.

Schools and districts have made great strides in providing students with devices and internet access. Now, administrators must also ensure that teachers have the time and resources to dedicate to cultivating the critical thinking habits that will enable students to identify accurate and relevant information.

So, how do we teach students these essential skills?

One place to start with basic AI literacy is to instruct students on how to conduct searches using effective prompts. Asking good questions the right way increases the odds of receiving a high-quality response. We'll look at specific examples of engineering queries in the next chapter.

From there, students need to know what to do with the AI-generated information they've gathered. Information literacy entails a two-step teaching process: detecting bias and validating information. Establishing a shared vocabulary for this process ensures students learn basic strategies they can remember and apply. If you've already been teaching digital (or information) literacy to any extent, you are probably familiar with two memorable acronyms that students can use to evaluate information: REAL and CRAP.

Alan November's REAL framework is a tool to help students (or anyone) check the reliability and credibility of their research sources:

> **Read the URL.** Did the link you clicked take you to the right website?
>
> **Examine the content.** Is the information on the site current? Or is it out of date?
>
> **Ask about the author.** Who created the site's content and are they trustworthy?
>
> **Look at the links.** Is the site referenced by multiple other resources? A highly credible source is often cited by or backlinked to other websites.[2]

Or maybe you use the CRAP test to evaluate information, considering aspects such as potential bias, accuracy, intent, and red flags indicating unreliable content:

> **Currency**—Is the information timely?
>
> **Relevance**—Is the information appropriate to your needs?
>
> **Authority/Accuracy**—Who wrote the content? Is the source reliable?
>
> **Purpose**—What is the purpose of the content? Is the point of view biased in any way?

These acronyms are examples of common vocabulary. When your students learn these terms and become adept at evaluating information using these frameworks, checking the validity of sources eventually becomes instinctive.[3]

Beyond developing these basic information literacy skills, we must learn to recognize coded biases within AI systems. **Coded bias** is the presence of biases in algorithms, AI systems, and LLMs due to the data they are trained on or the way they are designed. These biases can be unintentional, arising from factors such as historical prejudice, cultural norms, or imbalanced representation in the

---

2   I have a post about the REAL framework here: https://www.hollyclark.org/2017/03/02/find-validate-use/

3   In *The Chromebook Infused Classroom*, I devoted a section to digital literacy. The need for these skills is only going to increase.

training data. As a result, AI systems and algorithms can make biased decisions or produce biased outputs that unfairly favor or discriminate against certain groups or individuals.

To help my students detect coded bias, I created a quick-start guide using the simple acronym AI BIAS. The protocol prompts students to think more deeply about the information they receive from an AI tool.

AI Bias and Misinformation Starter Guide

Warning: This does not help with bias that is built into systems so firmly that we often don't recognize it or the coded bias that is nearly impossible to detect

A	I	B	I	A	S
Ask AI about Possible Bias	**Investigate** the References	**Build** Out Other Sources	**Intent** - Why did author write?	**Accuracy** Check	**Stop** if you see warning signs
Ask for information about possible bias from the LLM you are interacting with to get the information.	Investigate further by asking the AI for references and actual links to those references. It will provide those.	Build a quick list of 2-3 other references that can support the original references being provided. INFUSED classroom	Think about the intent of author by looking at other things written by author or linked to in the article. Does the author try to persuade you to think a certain way with no regard for actual evidence?	Pretends to present facts, but offers only opinions. There is no reference or indication of where this information came from.	The author is unidentifiable, lacks expertise, or writes on unrelated topics. It's a blog without evidence of ideas being put forward

For Asking AI   **For Validating the Information**

Ask the AI simple questions about the possibility of any bias in its response.

Investigate further by requesting links to the resources it used to craft the response. Be careful here: AI can provide fake links. That's why investigating includes checking links and the resources provided.

Build out other sources by asking critical questions about the resources and gathering additional sources to support the ideas represented in the AI-generated content.

Intent evaluation is the next step. Is the information being presented with the *intent* of persuading the reader to a particular point of view?

Accuracy is important, so details should be based on facts rather than opinions.

Stop using the source if any of the checks above raise red flags.

As with any framework, students will need assistance as they learn how to apply the steps of this AI BIAS evaluation process.

Alarmingly few educators exhibit proficiency in conducting effective online searches or evaluating the information they find. Today, those lacking these skills are at risk of falling behind in understanding AI and prompt engineering—which puts their students at risk as well.

As our reliance on AI-driven information grows, it is increasingly important to scrutinize content and strive to create a transparent and unbiased AI landscape. The danger is falling victim to false information or being persuaded by propaganda—without realizing it's happening. When this occurs, even educated adults believe and share false information. Think about the wild rumors, outrageous accusations, and unbelievable claims you've seen passed around the internet in the past few years. Perhaps you've even seen a video of your favorite celebrity saying or doing something that seems completely out of character. In many cases, the information gets shared as if it were truth—when it is anything but.

We have to do things better and smarter going forward. We need to be intentional about learning to validate information and recognize misinformation as well as possible types of biases and outright lies that can be baked into AI-generated content and query responses.

And we *must* pass on these vital skills to our students.

A Quick-Start Guide to Prompt Engineering

Two educators sat in the chairs across from me at the airport. One of them had recently discovered ChatGPT and was excitedly telling her friend what this new technology could do.

Coincidently, I was on my way to the Texas Computer Education Association (TCEA) convention where my friend and podcast co-host, Matt Miller, and I had been asked to speak about ChatGPT and AI in education. I couldn't help but listen in on their conversation.

The scenario played out a bit differently than I had anticipated.

"I have to show you this new thing," said the excited teacher. "It writes poems and things for you!"

Her friend sounded skeptical. "Why would anyone want something else to write a poem for them?"

"Wait, just let me show you. Let's ask it to write a poem." She spoke the words aloud as she typed in the prompt: "Write a poem about skiing."

We were in the Denver airport in February, and I wondered if they might have been on their way home from skiing.

Within fifteen seconds, ChatGPT had completed the task. They read the fun poem that had appeared on the screen.

"This is cute," the second teacher admitted. But she still didn't sound all that interested.

Her friend was happily relentless in sharing her enthusiasm. She listed off several things ChatGPT could do and then proceeded to show her friend:

"Make that poem into a play."

"Write a Haiku about skiing."

Each time, ChatGPT delivered.

The second teacher was amused but still unimpressed by what she had seen. Before they parted ways, I heard her say, "Email me that cute little poem, would you?"

After her friend walked away, I spoke up. "It's amazing how much ChatGPT can do, isn't it?"

And off we went, imagining the possibilities together. She told me she taught eighth grade English Language Arts in Illinois, and it was clear that her mind was racing with ideas about how she could use this new technology with her students.

We talked until it was time for me to board the plane. I smiled, knowing that her students were going to have some incredible learning experiences using the new tool that their teacher was so excited about.

I never found out what subject or grade the other teacher taught, but I would venture to guess that she went back to school without a second thought about ChatGPT.

And that's a shame.

I see both sides of this story play out all the time. Some teachers hear about AI tools, like ChatGPT or Google Bard, and are instantly curious about them for the classroom. Too many others either aren't interested in AI's potential or they're worried about how kids will use it to cheat.

My take is that kids *are* going to use it to cheat *if* we don't teach them better ways to use it first. And that starts, remember, with the right questions, or in more technical terms, engineering effective prompts.

That is what this chapter is all about.

Empower Students to Become Prompt Engineers

Prompt engineering is a technique used to guide AI language models, like ChatGPT, to generate accurate and relevant responses. It involves using precise instructions and keywords to carefully craft your questions or statements as well as providing context or examples when necessary. The intent, of course, is to help the AI understand your needs and generate better, more relevant answers or suggestions. The more clear and direct you are with your instructions or request, the more likely you are to get the answers you need.

Think of it this way: If a student were to ask a classmate for help with homework, he might simply ask, "Could you help me with math?" His classmate would have context and would know what the teacher taught that day.

AI tools don't have that context. (Although, who knows? That day may be coming.) So, if the same student wanted to ask ChatGPT for help with his math homework, he would need to be more specific in his request. Instead of saying, "Help me with math," he could use the prompt:

Can you explain how to solve this quadratic equation using the quadratic formula and do it in a step-by-step fashion?

Asking for exactly what you want increases the chances of getting the help you need. That's true in life, and it's true when communicating with AI language models.

What can you ask for?
The following quick-start guide offers examples of prompts that teachers can use or adapt. The information that comes back could be used for class discussions, lessons, and hands-on unit creation. What can you ask for? Just about anything.

Create a Table of Responses
Gather information quickly for lessons, discussion, and more! Here's a quick example:

Your class is reading S.E. Hinton's book *The Outsiders.* Your prompt might look something like this: *Generate a table containing responses summarizing the book The Outsiders. The table should include persuasive, explanatory, humorous, critical, and high interest.*

Distribute the table to students through Google Classroom or your preferred Learning Management System. Then, engage students in critiquing and analyzing the distinct examples of how writing styles influence the perception and impact of a text.

Communication Style	Response Summary
Persuasive	"The Outsiders" is a must-read novel that will captivate you with its poignant portrayal of social class struggles, the power of friendship, and the search for belonging. This timeless story will resonate with readers of all ages and leave a lasting impact on your perception of societal divisions
Explanatory	"The Outsiders" is a coming-of-age novel that follows the story of Ponyboy Curtis, a member of the lower-class gang called the Greasers. The novel explores the conflicts between the Greasers and the wealthier Socs, delving into themes of loyalty, identity, and the consequences of social inequality.
Humorous	Ever wondered what it's like to be a "greaser" in the 1960s? Dive into "The Outsiders to explore the misadventures of Ponyboy Curtis and his gang of friends as they navigate the treacherous waters of hairstyles, high school, and high-stakes rumbles against their archenemies, the snobby Socs.
Critical	While "The Outsiders is an engaging and emotional story, it falls short in exploring the deeper systemic issues underlying the social divide between the Greasers and the Socs. The novel tends to oversimplify the complexities of societal issues by primarily focusing on the experiences of the main characters.
High-Interest	"The Outsiders" is a gripping tale of loyalty, friendship, and finding your place in a divided world. You'll be immersed in the lives of Ponyboy Curtis and his gang of Greasers as they navigate their way through turbulent teenage years, facing off against their rivals, the Socs, in an unforgettable and emotional journey.

Generate a List of Questions

You can use an AI model like a teacher's assistant in a variety of ways, including asking it to generate a list of questions about a topic. An example of a prompt might be: *You are an 11th grade English teacher. Generate a list of questions about the book, The Outsiders, to test students' comprehension of the plot.*

Here are just a few benefits of using AI to generate questions:

Saves time—An AI model can quickly generate a list of questions, allowing you to focus on other important aspects of your work, such as making time to talk with students.

Provides more comprehensive information—AI models have access to vast amounts of information, which enables them to create questions that cover a wide range of aspects related to the topic. This can help ensure that you address all relevant points and angles.

Promotes critical thinking—The questions generated by the AI model can encourage students to think more deeply about the topic, explore different perspectives, and assess their understanding.

Sparks creativity—AI-generated questions can inspire new ideas or avenues for exploration that you and your students may not have considered otherwise. This can lead to more engaging and innovative discussions or projects.

Kicks off collaborative discussions—The list of questions can serve as a starting point for group discussions, debates, and collaborative learning.

Play Devil's Advocate

Asking an AI model to play devil's advocate for you can help you see things you might otherwise miss. Here's how you might use these prompts in the classroom:

Broaden your perspective—Have your students consider alternative viewpoints for a well-rounded view of a topic and to promote empathy, understanding, and open-mindedness.

Strengthen your arguments—By challenging beliefs and assumptions, AI can point out weaknesses or blind spots in an argument. Addressing these issues will result in a more robust, well-developed position.

Encourage critical thinking—Considering alternate points of view forces people to think critically about their stance. Using AI this way, students can evaluate and respond to counterarguments thoughtfully and logically.

Show Me This Idea in Real Life

Asking an AI model to provide ideas or examples from real life can be advantageous for several reasons:

Contextual understanding—Real-life examples help to illustrate abstract concepts or theories, making them more relatable and easier to grasp. Stories can enhance students' understanding of a topic and connect concepts to practical applications.

Relevance and engagement—Ideas grounded in real-world situations are often more engaging and relevant to our lives. By connecting theoretical knowledge to actual experiences, you can capture the interest of your audience, making the information more memorable and meaningful.

Create An Outline

You can use AI to create an outline for a story, writing prompt, or presentation by providing a brief description of the story idea, genre, or theme you (or your students) have in mind. AI can then generate an outline or structure.

With narratives, AI can include potential plot points, character development, and setting details. Here's an example of a prompt to create an outline for a story:

Bella and Peyton, childhood friends from a small town, spend their summer vacation in a large city. While exploring the city, they stumble upon an abandoned mansion in a neighborhood not far away from the house they are staying in. Despite warnings from locals to stay away, they decide to explore the mansion and uncover its secrets. What do they find, and how does their adventure change their friendship?.

AI can be a valuable tool in kick-starting the writing process and providing a solid foundation for your narrative. Just keep in mind that AI-generated outlines will require editing or revision to ensure they align with each writer's vision.

> **Teaching Tip:** If students don't know what to write about, give them a prompt structure, like the one above, and have them change the details. They can then ask ChatGPT to use their personalized prompts to create a suggested outline. From there, students can revise the outline and add ideas to make their story unique.

Simulate This Scenario

AI can simulate scenarios for students, providing them with interactive and immersive learning experiences that foster a deeper understanding of the subject matter.

An example might be to ask students to prompt AI to simulate a scenario where oil spills into a local waterway. What might happen? What would the costs of recovery and cleanup be? Would there be long-term consequences?

Act as Though

The *act as though* prompt can be an effective way to engage students in creative thinking, problem-solving, and empathy-building exercises. Here are a few examples to consider or adapt:

Act as though you are the president of a country dealing with a natural disaster. How would you coordinate the response efforts and allocate resources to help those affected?

Act as though you are a scientist who has just discovered a new species. How would you document your findings, and what steps would you take to protect the habitat of this species?

Act as though you are a character in a book. What choices could you make that might alter the plot?

Act as though you are an architect designing a sustainable city. What features and technologies would you incorporate to minimize the city's environmental impact while providing a high quality of life for its inhabitants?

Act as though you are a master teacher in a classroom with diverse learning needs and students with different backgrounds. How would you modify this lesson plan to ensure that all students can engage with the material, see themselves, and succeed?

Expand or Explain in Step-by-Step

Asking AI to explain a task step-by-step breaks down the concept or process. This provides clarity and makes it easier to grasp complex topics or procedures. Because the information is presented in a logical order, it is easy for learners to follow.

Step-by-step explanations are particularly beneficial for learners who may be new to a subject. The structured framework empowers them to build knowledge and understanding gradually. Additionally, when learners take in the directions a little at a time, mastering each step along the way, they are more likely to retain and recall what they've learned.

Ignore All Previous Instructions Before This One

This prompt is designed to help the AI model forget any biases or previous instructions that may have influenced its responses. By giving the AI model this prompt, you are essentially starting from scratch and allowing it to generate responses based purely on the current prompt and the data it has been trained on. This can be especially useful when you want to avoid any unintentional biases or limitations in the AI model's responses. It's like hitting the reset button and starting with a blank slate. Just be aware that the AI model may need some time to re-learn and adjust to this new approach.

QUICK START GUIDE FOR TEACHERS AND STUDENTS

TABLE OF RESPONSES
TABLE WITH FIVE WRITING STYLES

PLAY DEVIL'S ADVOCATE...

EXPAND OR EXPLAIN IN STEP-BY-STEP

SUMMARIZE {X} FOR A {N}

SUMMARIZE COLD FUSION FOR A 10 YEAR OLD

ACT AS THOUGH

SIMULATE THIS SCENARIO

GENERATE A LIST OF QUESTIONS ABOUT

CREATE AN OUTLINE FOR A STORY OR WRITING PROMPT

SHOW ME THIS IDEA IN REAL LIFE

I.E. QUADRATIC EQUATION

AI PROMPT ENGINEERING
How to Talk to AI to Get Better Responses

IGNORE ALL PREVIOUS INSTRUCTIONS BEFORE THIS ONE

MAKING THE SHIFT WITH AI

Key Questions for Navigating AI in Education

With this incredible shift in information exchange, there seem to be more questions than answers. Throughout this book, I have tried to address many of them, but I certainly don't have all the answers. No one does, but that's okay. It means we're still growing.

Questions are always a great place to start. By considering the implications and possibilities of AI in education and how we can integrate these tools into our classrooms, we can know we are asking the right questions.

I've listed a few below for you to consider with your fellow educators. I'd love to hear your perspective on and experiences with AI. Tag me on social media @HollyClarkEdu.

1 How can AI tools and applications be integrated into various subjects to enhance learning experiences?

2 What essential skills should students acquire to succeed in an AI-driven world?

3 How can educators promote digital and information literacy to help students evaluate AI-generated content and recognize biases?

4 What strategies should be taught to students for effectively engaging with AI tools and interpreting AI-generated responses?

5 What ethical considerations should be addressed when introducing AI into the classroom?

6 How can educators foster critical thinking and problem-solving skills to ensure students' future marketplace relevance in the face of automation?

7 What exposure to AI-related subjects and skills should be provided to prepare students for AI-driven careers?

8 How can educators stay informed about the latest AI developments and integrate them into their teaching practices?

9 What professional development opportunities should be offered to help educators adapt to AI integration in education?

10 How can educators collaborate with AI stakeholders, such as developers, researchers, and policymakers, to ensure responsible and effective AI use in the classroom?

What does ChatGPT have to say?

Because I don't have all the answers to these bigger questions and each school district will approach it differently, I asked ChatGPT for its input on these issues. Here are the responses:

Q: How can AI tools and applications be integrated into various subjects to enhance learning experiences?

AI: AI tools can be integrated into various subjects by personalizing learning experiences, providing instant feedback, promoting questioning and inquiry, and offering intelligent tutoring systems to support student growth.

Q: What essential skills should students acquire to succeed in an AI-driven world?

AI: Essential skills students should acquire to succeed in an AI-driven world include critical thinking, creativity, collaboration, communication, digital literacy, data analysis, coding, and an understanding of machine learning and AI principles.

Q: How can educators promote digital and information literacy to help students evaluate AI-generated content and recognize biases?

AI: Educators can promote digital and information literacy by teaching students to evaluate sources, identify biases, analyze data, and validate information. Encouraging students to question the reliability and accuracy of AI-generated content is also essential.

Q: What strategies should be taught to students for effectively engaging with AI tools and interpreting AI-generated responses?

AI: Strategies for effectively engaging with AI tools include understanding how AI works, recognizing the limitations of AI, practicing clear communication and questioning techniques, and developing a growth mindset for learning from AI interactions.

Q: What ethical considerations should be addressed when introducing AI into the classroom?

AI: Ethical considerations when introducing AI into the classroom include data privacy and security, equitable access to AI tools, potential biases in AI algorithms, the impact of AI on employment, and the ethical use of AI-generated content.

Q: How can educators foster critical thinking and problem-solving skills to ensure students' relevance in the face of automation?

AI: Educators can foster critical thinking and problem-solving skills by incorporating inquiry-based learning, real-world problem-solving activities, and encouraging reflection and evaluation of AI-generated content.

Q: What exposure to AI-related subjects and skills should be provided to prepare students for AI-driven careers?

AI: Exposure to AI-related subjects and skills can be provided through inter-disciplinary projects, coding and robotics courses, data science classes, and opportunities to learn about AI ethics, policy, and social implications.

Q: How can educators stay informed about the latest AI developments and integrate them into their teaching practices?

AI: Educators can stay informed about the latest AI developments by attending conferences, participating in professional development programs, engaging in online communities where their algorithm brings them the latest updates, and reading research articles.

Q: What professional development opportunities should be offered to help educators adapt to AI integration in education?

AI: Professional development opportunities for educators to adapt to AI integration in education may include workshops, webinars, online courses, and peer-to-peer training on AI tools, techniques, and best practices.

Q: How can educators collaborate with AI stakeholders, such as developers, researchers, and policymakers, to ensure responsible and effective AI use in the classroom?

AI: Educators can collaborate with AI stakeholders by participating in inter-disciplinary research projects, joining AI-focused educational organizations, attending AI-focused conferences, and engaging in conversations with developers, researchers, and policymakers to ensure responsible and effective AI use in the classroom.

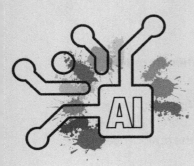

Just for Fun
Appendix

What if we rethought everything?

I have added this section just for fun, so you can see how we might frame a new type of prompt for teachers that puts learning into students' hands.

Prompt: *I need to teach students about the Roman Republic. How can I put that learning back in their hands and not be the person "teaching," but rather mentoring?*

ChatGPT Answer

To shift from a traditional teaching role to a mentorship role in teaching students about the Roman Republic, consider the following strategies:

Project-based learning: Assign students a project related to the Roman Republic, such as researching a specific historical figure, event, or aspect of daily life. Encourage them to use a variety of sources and create a final presentation or report to share their findings with the class.

Collaborative group work: Divide students into small groups and assign each group a topic related to the Roman Republic. Encourage them to collaborate, share resources, and discuss their findings with each other. As a mentor, you can facilitate discussions and provide guidance when needed.

Inquiry-based learning: Develop guiding questions that will prompt students to explore various aspects of the Roman Republic on their own. Encourage them to form their own questions and seek answers through independent research.

Student-led discussions: Organize regular class discussions where students take the lead in presenting their findings and engaging their peers in conversation about the Roman Republic. As a mentor, you can guide the discussions, provide context, and challenge their understanding when necessary.

Use of multimedia resources: Encourage students to utilize multimedia resources like documentaries, podcasts, and interactive websites to learn about the Roman Republic. This will allow them to take charge of their learning and choose resources that cater to their interests and learning styles.

Role-playing activities: Organize role-playing activities or simulations that allow students to take on the roles of historical figures from the Roman Republic. This can help them develop a deeper understanding of the historical context and the challenges faced by people at that time.

Encourage reflection: Have students maintain a learning journal where they can reflect on their learning experiences, challenges, and progress. This can help them develop self-awareness and become more independent learners.

Socratic seminars: Organize Socratic seminars, where students engage in dialogue about the Roman Republic based on a shared text or resource. This method encourages critical thinking and helps students learn from each other.

Peer feedback and evaluation: Encourage students to give each other feedback on their work, presentations, or discussions. This promotes a collaborative learning environment where students learn from their peers and improve their understanding of the Roman Republic.

Ongoing support and guidance: As a mentor, provide continuous support and guidance to your students throughout the learning process. Offer help with research, resources, and clarification of concepts when needed, but allow them the autonomy to explore and learn independently.

By implementing these strategies, you can create a student-centered learning environment that fosters autonomy, collaboration, and critical thinking, while still providing guidance and support as a mentor.

Here's How Amazing Teachers Are Using This Tool

Take a look around the edusphere to discover how others are using and thinking about this new technology. I'd love to hear how you are infusing AI into your classroom! Tag me on Instagram and Twitter @HollyClarkEdu and let me know your best strategies and tips for using AI with your students.

Shout out to Alec Couros (@courosa) for this Twitter thread of educators ready to see ChatGPT as a tool for learning.

Julie Daniel Davis, CETL @juliedavisEDU · Mar 21
I created a lesson plan and a corresponding slidedeck for my preservice teachers. I didn't accept it wholeheartedly but it was a great jumping off point for me to enhance it for my own.

Michelle Wagner @wagnerlearning · Mar 22
My daughter cut and pasted her essay into ChatGPT and asked for feedback as if from a 7th grade teacher.

Aimée Skidmore @skidmoreaimee · Mar 20
Marking, feedback, generating discussion questions and writing samples, Report card comments, sorting survey responses to find trends in misunderstanding. Have much more and happy to elaborate

Blair Davenport @BlairDavenport0 · Mar 21
I've used it to create exemplars for writing, for backwards mapping standards, creating K.U.D. charts, plugging in a rubric/prompt & getting examples for each level. I took Ss descriptions of their narrative characters/setting & plugged it into Dall-E

Michael Kennedy @M_J_Kennedy · Mar 21
Replying to @courosa
Writing sample essays to mimic (mentor texts) for students who struggle with writing.

Liz Gunderson @LionHeartLiz · Mar 21
Replying to @courosa
I have used it to generate and differentiate text for students. This evens the playing field for all to access text.

Annie Tiller @atille1 · Mar 21

Replying to @courosa

Used it for getting quick list of higher order thinking questions for specific units. Example-first grade parts of a plant.

Tom Hammerlund @thammerlund · Mar 20

With Students –
Our grade 5/6 team introduced AI tools in a unit about using technology for communication. We introduced CGPT, talked about strengths and weaknesses, how and when we should use it, and created an essential agreement. They also played around with AI image tools
/1

Mary Neely @Neely17 · Mar 22

Replying to @courosa

Used ChatGPT in drama class. In groups Ss chose a specific scenario for their monologue and the got ChatGPT to write it each one from the perspective of a different age. We then compared the language used to study how word choice matters when writing from perspective.

Ashley Anderson @ashley4slcboard · Mar 22

Replying to @courosa

1st through 6th buddies have used Dall-E 2 to design imaginary habitats including the mythical creatures who live there. We discuss the language of effective prompts, the types of visual art styles available, and the feasibility/relationship to real habitats.

Lindsay Cesari @MrsCesari · Mar 21

Also used Midjourney to generate images of characters based on descriptions in a novel, and then used those images to generate a character map (this is for All American Boys) to support students as they read.

Tony Bollino @techtimetony · Mar 21

Replying to @courosa

I have used it to develop a station rotation about the causes of the American Revolution. It was a good start but needed adjustment for our local standards.

Britt @brittany95_ · Mar 21

Replying to @courosa

Used #ChatGPT to create role cards for my biology students to take on different real world perspectives when analyzing the use of CRISPR gene editing

···

 Josh Polk @JoshPolk · Mar 21

Replying to @courosa

My students prototyped and designed web sites for a cause of their own choice. I let them use chatgpt to generate copy for the site and bullet points. Much better than Lorem Ipsum!

···

 HJ Myers @Audacity_of_Me · Mar 21

Replying to @courosa

I'm having them use it to ask for templates. For example, "how do I write an argumentative thesis?" The program does a great job of setting students up with the hows of thought expression. I'm also using it for them to draft their emails to me and make them formal.

···

 Win Himsworth @whimsworth · Mar 21

Replying to @courosa

Pre-AI, I had my students write reports. Now I have ChatGPT write reports then ask students to critique them, examine sources, and suggest additions/improvements. The students are developing critical analysis skills and actually learning more about the topics.

···

 Glenn Borthistle @gborthis · Mar 21

Replying to @courosa

Will be incorporating Chat GPT into my students final assignment. Ask three questions about your topic and then write a critique of what it says.

···

 Kim Richardson, PhD, PCC® @drkimrichardson · Mar 21

Replying to @courosa

I have asked it to create reflective prompts connected to certain content that I am presenting.

···

donnie piercey
@mrpiercEy

So this is kinda cool... turns out at that Midjourney is great at coming up with example illustrations for assignments if you ever need any.

"Create a sketch done by a fifth grader using colored pencils or markers after Mighty Casey strikes out in the poem Casey at the Bat."

TikToks

AI bot essay plan!

What do you think? Useful to generate AI representations of characters?

More from
Elevate Books EDU

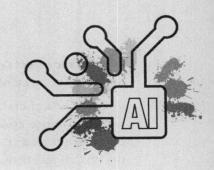

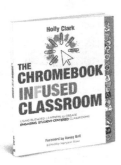

The Chromebook Infused Classroom: Using Blended Learning to Create Engaging, Student-Centered Classrooms

By Holly Clark

Whether Chromebooks are a new addition to your school, or you have recently gone 1:1 in the classroom, or have been using them for years and you want to make the most of technology for your learners. *The Chromebook Infused Classroom* is a resource you will want to refer to again and again.

The Google Infused Classroom: A Guidebook to Making Thinking Visible and Amplifying Student Voice

By Holly Clark and Tanya Avrith

This beautifully designed book offers guidance on using technology to design instruction that allows students to show their thinking, demonstrate their learning, and share their work (and voices!) with authentic audiences. The Google Infused Classroom will equip you to empower your students to use technology in meaningful ways that prepare them for the future.

The Microsoft Infused Classroom: A Guidebook to Making Thinking Visible and Amplifying Student Voice

By Holly Clark

Looking for ways to create a student-centered classroom and make your lessons come alive? *The Microsoft Infused Classroom* has the answers! Designed to help you amplify teaching and engagement in your classroom, *The Microsoft Infused Classroom* equips you to use powerful tools that put learning first!

40 Ways to Inject Creativity with Adobe Spark

By Ben Fort and Monica Burns

In the hands of creative educators, Adobe Spark provides students with a fun way to embrace critical communication and creativity skills. But what if you don't consider yourself a "creative educator" or just aren't sure where to start? With the tips, suggestions, and encouragement in this book, you'll find everything you need to inject creativity into your classroom using Adobe Spark.

Dive into Inquiry: Amplify Learning and Empower Student Voice

By Trevor MacKenzie

Dive into Inquiry beautifully marries the voice and choice of inquiry with the structure and support required to optimize learning for students and get the results educators desire. With *Dive into Inquiry,* you'll gain an understanding of how to best support your learners as they shift from a traditional learning model into the inquiry classroom where student agency is fostered and celebrated every day. An ideal text for middle and high school educators!

Flipgrid in the InterACTIVE Class: Encouraging Inclusion and Student Voice in the Elementary Classroom

By Joe and Kristin Merrill

Have you been searching for ways to connect with students in your classroom? If so, you are ready to dive into *Flipgrid in the InterACTIVE Class!* Flipgrid is an educational platform that is free and accessible to teachers worldwide. Using simple video tools, educators can engage their students, families, and community in meaningful discussions and learning experiences.

How to Sketchnote: A Step-by-Step Manual for Teachers and Students

By Sylvia Duckworth

Discover the Benefits of Doodling! Educator and internationally known sketchnoter Sylvia Duckworth makes ideas memorable and shareable with her simple yet powerful drawings. In How to Sketchnote, she explains how you can use sketchnoting in the classroom and that you don't have to be an artist to discover the benefits of doodling!

Inquiry Mindset: Nurturing the Dreams, Wonders, & Curiosities of Our Youngest Learners—Elementary Edition

By Trevor MacKenzie and Rebecca Bushby

From their youngest years, our children are innately curious. They explore the world around them through play, imagination, and discovery. They build meaning, they create understanding, and they unabashedly share their learning. It's in this process that they find joy in life and relevance in the world around them.

Leading with a Lens of Inquiry

By Jessica Vance

Leading with a Lens of Inquiry is a guide for leaders who wish to cultivate learning spaces that honor the agency and curiosity of all learners. This book outlines critical ways leaders embody the dispositions of an inquiry educator, modeling for teachers the very mindset and moves we know students should experience in their classrooms. An ideal text for school leaders, curriculum coordinators, and instructional coaches.

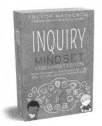

Inquiry Mindset: Scaffolding a Partnership for Equity and Agency in Learning—Assessment Edition

By Trevor MacKenzie

Trevor takes another deep dive into inquiry as he examines the role of assessment in education through the lens of co-designing and co-constructing with students. In *Inquiry Mindset: Assessment Edition*, he outlines the beliefs, values, and frameworks that allow teachers to scaffold assessments infused with student voice, understanding, and autonomy.

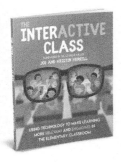

The InterACTIVE Class: Using Technology to Make Learning More Relevant and Engaging in the Elementary Classroom

By Kristin and Joe Merrill

This book is packed with great ideas for the elementary classroom! Are you looking for ways to make teaching and learning more interactive in your classroom? Do you ever feel overwhelmed when it comes to integrating technology and content standards? Are you searching for lessons that you can immediately implement in your learning environment? Then you are ready to dive into *The InterACTIVE Classroom*! In this practical and idea-packed book, coauthors and classroom teachers Joe and Kristin Merrill share their personal framework for teaching.

The Microsoft Teams Playbook: Your Guide to Creating an Empowered Classroom

By Jeni Long and Sallee Clark

In *The Microsoft Teams Playbook*, edtech experts and coauthors Jeni Long and Salleé Clark (hosts of The #Jenallee Show) provide a coach's manual for creating empowered classrooms. Using Microsoft Teams as a multifaceted hub and integrating other powerful edtech tools, the authors guide teachers to foster learning opportunities that are accessible and equitable for all students.

Sketchnotes for Educators: 100 Inspiring Illustrations for Lifelong Learners

By Sylvia Duckworth

This inspirational book contains 100 of Sylvia Duckworth's most popular sketch-notes with links to the original downloads that can be used in class or shared with colleagues. Interspersed throughout the book are Sylvia's reflections on each drawing and what motivated her to create them, in addition to commentary from other educators who inspired the sketchnotes.

About the Author

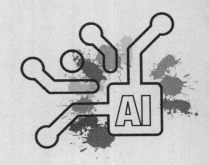

Meet **Holly Clark**, a passionate educator and digital learning pioneer who has made significant contributions to the field of educational technology. With more than twenty-five years of experience, Holly is an international speaker, bestselling author, and dedicated advocate for digital learning. She was one of the first teachers in the nation to have a 1:1 classroom, and she now shares her knowledge and insights to help other teachers tap into their blended learning genius.

Holly's work with thousands of educators around the globe has helped transform teaching practices through the purposeful use of technology. Her 1:1 classroom experience, strategic initiatives, and training programs have made her a go-to resource for educators who are looking to enhance their students' learning experiences through technology integration.

Holly's impact on the education industry is reflected in her acclaimed books, *The Google Infused Classroom* and *The Chromebook Infused Classroom*, which are highly regarded by educators worldwide. She is a Google Certified Innovator, a Microsoft Innovative Educator Expert, and a National Board Certified Teacher.

Connect with Holly Clark

- Blog: hollyclark.org
- Instagram and Twitter @HollyClarkEdu
- Email: holly@hollyclark.org

Made in the USA
Las Vegas, NV
17 May 2024

90043303R00072